easy knitting
Chic

easy knitting
Chic

30 projects to make for your home and to wear

Consultant: Nikki Trench

hamlyn

An Hachette UK Company
www.hachette.co.uk

First published in Great Britain in 2013 by
Hamlyn, a division of Octopus Publishing Group Ltd
Endeavour House
189 Shaftesbury Avenue
London
WC2H 8JY
www.octopusbooks.co.uk

ISBN 978-0-600-62829-3

A CIP catalogue record for this book is available from the
British Library

Printed and bound in China

10 9 8 7 6 5 4 3 2 1

Contents

Introduction

If you can knit a few basic stitches, you can create stylish knitted items to wear, use to decorate your home and give as gifts for friends and family.

Whether you are a relative beginner, a confident convert or a long-term aficionado, there are projects here to delight. While your first attempts may be a bit uneven, a little practice and experimentation will ensure you soon improve. None of the projects here is beyond the scope of even those fairly new to the hobby.

Knitting has justifiably lost its fusty image – with the right patterns you can create some really chic clothing and smart accessories for you and your home. Whatever your tastes and experience, there is much to choose from here, from cardigans and scarves to bags and cushions/pillows. All would make charming, unique gifts.

Knitting essentials

All you really need to get knitting is a pair of needles and some yarn. For some projects, that's it; for others additional items are required, most of which can be found in a fairly basic sewing kit. All measurements are given in metric and imperial. Choose which to work in and stick with it since conversions may not be exact.

- **Needles** These come in metric (mm), British and US sizes and are made from different materials, all of which affect the weight and 'feel' of the needles – which you choose is down to personal preference. Circular and double-pointed needles are sometimes used as well.
- **Yarns** Specific yarns are listed for each project, but full details of the yarn's composition and the ball lengths are given so that you can choose alternatives, either from online sources or from your local supplier, many of whom have very knowledgeable staff. Do keep any leftover yarns (not forgetting the ball bands, since these contain vital information) to use for future projects.
- **Additional items**: Some projects require making up and finishing, and need further materials or equipment, such as sewing needles, buttons and other accessories. These are detailed in each project's Getting Started box.

What is in this book

All projects are illustrated with several photographs to show you the detail of the work – both inspirational and useful for reference. A full summary of each project is given in the Getting Started box so you can see exactly what's involved. Here, projects are graded from one ball of yarn (straightforward, suitable for beginners) through two (more challenging) to three balls (for knitters with more confidence and experience).

Also in the Getting Started box is the size of each finished item, yarn(s), needles and additional items needed, and what tension/gauge the project is worked in. Finally, a breakdown of the steps involved is given so you know exactly what the project entails before you start.

At the beginning of the pattern instructions is a key to all abbreviations that are used in that project, while occasional notes expand on the pattern instructions where necessary.

If you have enjoyed the projects here, you may want to explore the other titles in the Easy Knitting series: *Babies & Children*, *Cosy*, *Country*, *Vintage & Retro* and *Weekend*. For those who enjoy crochet, a sister series, Easy Crochet, features similarly stylish yet simple projects.

Metric	British	US
2 mm	14	0
2.5 mm	13	1
2.75 mm	12	2
3mm	11	n/a
3.25 mm	10	3
3.5 mm	n/a	4
3.75 mm	9	5
4 mm	8	6
4.5 mm	7	7
5 mm	6	8
5.5 mm	5	9
6 mm	4	10
6.5 mm	3	10.5
7 mm	2	n/a
7.5 mm	1	n/a
8 mm	0	11
9 mm	0	13
10 mm	0	15

Wrap-around cardigan

Worked in a soft yarn and lightly textured stitch, this wrap-around jacket will keep you snug on chilly days.

The front of this soft and cuddly unstructured jacket can be left to hang loose or can be fastened with a pin or brooch.

GETTING STARTED

Fronts and back worked in one piece with cast/bound-off and cast-on stitches for armhole openings. The sleeves are shaped with simple increases

Size:

To fit bust: 76–81[81–86:91–97:102–107]cm/ 30–32[32–34:36–38:40–42]in

Actual size bust (with front overlapped): 85[96.5:108:120]cm/33½[38:42½:47¼]in

Length (including collar): 55.5[60.5:65:70] cm/22[24:25½:27½]in

Sleeve seam (with cuff turned back): 48cm (19in)

Note: Figures in square brackets [ ] refer to larger sizes; where there is only one set of figures, it applies to all sizes

How much yarn:

4[5:6:7] x 50g (2oz) balls of Rowan Kid Classic, approx 140m (153 yards) per ball

Needles:

Pair of 5mm (no. 6/US 8) needles

Tension/gauge:

17 stitches and 24 rows to 10cm (4in) over moss stitch on 5mm (no. 6/US 8) needles.

IT IS ESSENTIAL TO WORK TO THE STATED TENSION/ GAUGE TO ACHIEVE SUCCESS

What you have to do:

Cast on. Work in moss/seed stitch. Cast on and cast/ bind off stitches for armhole openings. Shape sleeves with simple increases. Cast/bind off.

Note: This very simple jacket is worked sideways. The fronts and back are all in one piece with openings left for the armholes, while the sleeves are added afterwards.

The Yarn

Rowan Kid Classic is a perfect blend of lambswool and 26% kid mohair so the finished fabric is very soft and cuddly. There are a range of muted and neutral shades and some subtle pastels.

 Instructions

Abbreviations:

alt = alternate;
cm = centimetre(s)
cont = continue;
foll = following;
inc = increase;
k = knit;
kfb = k into front and back of st;
p = purl; **patt** = pattern;
rep = repeat;
RS = right side;
st(s) = stitch(es);
WS = wrong side

FRONTS AND BACK:

Cast on 95[103:111:119] sts for right front.
1st row: (RS) P1, (k1, p1) to end.
Rep this row to form moss/seed st patt.
Cont in moss/seed st, work 77[83:89:95] more rows.

Shape right armhole:

Next row: (RS) Patt 21[23:25:27] sts, cast/
bind off next 33[37:41:45] sts loosely, patt
to end.
Cont on last set of 41[43:45:47] sts for
underarm. Work 10[14:18:22] rows moss/
seed st.
Next row: (WS) Patt 41[43:45:47] sts,
cast on 33[37:41:45] sts, patt to end.
95[103:111:119] sts.

Back:

Work 92[102:112:122] rows in moss/seed
st.

Shape left armhole:

Work as given for right armhole.

Left front:

Work 77[83:89:95] rows in moss/seed
st, ending with a RS row. Cast/bind off in
moss/seed st.

SLEEVES: (Make 2)

Cast on 41[45:49:53] sts. Work
44[40:38:44] rows in moss/seed st.
Next row: (inc row – RS) Kfb, patt to last
2 sts, kfb, k1. 43[47:51:55] sts.
Keeping patt correct, inc in this way at each
end of every foll 10th[10th:8th:6th] row
until there are 57[61:69:77] sts. Patt 3 rows.
Inc one st at each end of next and every
foll alt row until there are 67[75:83:91] sts.
Work 7[9:11:13] rows without shaping.
Cast/bind off loosely.

Tips

• Cast on for the armholes by looping
stitches on with your left thumb. If you
give each loop an extra twist before
putting it on the right needle, the edge
will be flexible but less loopy.
• After sewing up the garment, brush the
surface of the knitting lightly with a soft
brush to enhance the mohair effect.

Making up

Using backstitch, sew cast/bound-off edge of sleeve to cast/bound-off and cast-on edges of armhole opening, then sew row ends at tops of sleeves to row-ends at underarm. Join sleeve seams, reversing seam for about 5cm (2in) for turn-back cuff.

Red, white and black cushion

Simple colours and striking design give this cushion/pillow a hint of Japanese style.

Bold black and textured white stripes look striking on the front of this cushion/pillow, while the big red buttons echo the colour used for the back, which is knitted in another textured stitch.

GETTING STARTED

 Working intarsia stripes requires some practice

Size:
Cushion/pillow is 30cm x 40cm (12in x 16in)

How much yarn:
3 x 50g (2oz) balls of Debbie Bliss Rialto DK, approx 105m (115 yards) per ball, in colour A
2 balls in colour B
1 ball in colour C

Needles:
Pair of 4mm (no. 8/US 6) knitting needles

Additional items:
3 x 4.5cm (1¾in) red buttons
30cm x 40cm (12in x 16in) cushion pad/pillow form

Tension/gauge:
18 sts and 30 rows measure 10cm (4in) square over basketweave patt on 4mm (no. 8/US 6) needles
IT IS ESSENTIAL TO WORK TO THE STATED TENSION/GAUGE TO ACHIEVE SUCCESS

What you have to do:
Work back in basketweave pattern. Work front in vertical stripes with alternating stripes in stocking/ stockinette stitch and double moss/seed stitch. Use intarsia technique for stripes with small balls of yarn, twisting them together on wrong side of work when changing colour. Make cast/bound-off buttonholes in front edging.

The Yarn
Debbie Bliss Rialto DK is 100% extra fine merino wool. It gives good stitch definition for stocking/ stockinette stitch fabric and textured patterns and there are plenty of fabulous shades to choose from.

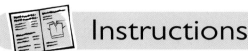

Instructions

BACK:

With A, cast on 67 sts. K 5 rows. Cont in basketweave patt as foll:

1st row: (RS) (K3, p3) to last st, k1.

2nd row: P1, (k3, p3) to end.

3rd row: As 1st row.

4th row: K1, (p3, k3) to end.

5th row: (P3, k3) to last st, p1.

6th row: As 4th row.

Rep these 6 rows to form patt until work measures 58cm (23in) from beg, ending with a WS row.

Cast/bind off in patt.

FRONT:

With B, cast on 67 sts. Work 6 rows as foll: p 1 row, k 1 row, p 2 rows and k 2 rows.

1st buttonhole row: (RS) P11, cast/bind off next 7 sts, (p until there are 12 sts on right needle after cast/bind off next 7 sts) twice, p to end.

2nd buttonhole row: K to end, casting on 7 sts over those cast/bound off in previous row.

Now work 6 rows as foll: (k 1 row and p 2 rows) twice.

Cont in stripe patt, using small separate balls of B and C for stripes and twisting yarns tog on WS of work when changing colour to avoid holes forming.

1st row: (RS) K14 B, 5 C, (12 B, 5 C) twice, 14 B.

2nd row: P14 B, k1 C, p1 C, k1 C, p1 C, k1 C, (p12 B, k1 C, p1 C, k1 C, p1 C, k1 C) twice, p14 B.

3rd row: K14 B, p1 C, k1 C, p1 C, k1 C, p1 C, (k12 B, p1 C, k1 C, p1 C, k1 C, p1 C) twice, k14 B.

4th row: P14 B, p1 C, k1 C, p1 C, k1 C, p1 C, (p12 B, p1 C, k1 C, p1 C, k1 C, p1 C) twice, p14 B.

5th row: K14 B, k1 C, p1 C, k1 C, p1 C, k1 C, (k12 B, k1 C, p1 C, k1 C, p1 C, k1 C) twice, k14 B.

Rep 2nd–5th rows throughout to form stripes of st st in B and double moss/seed st in C until work measures 43cm (17in) from beg, ending with a WS row.

With B only cast/bind off knitwise.

 ## Making up

Press according to directions on ball band. Place back and front tog with RS facing and leaving garter-stitch edging of back extended beyond buttonhole edging of front. Backstitch tog around three sides, leaving buttonhole-edge open. Fold extended back panel over onto front section (to form envelope opening) and overcast in place along side edge. Turn cushion/pillow cover RS out and sew on buttons to correspond with buttonholes. Insert cushion pad/pillow form and button cover closed.

Laptop bag

Knitted and then felted, this useful over-the-shoulder bag is practical and looks good, too.

Carry your laptop around in this funky, felted fabric holdall featuring distinctive intarsia stripes.

GETTING STARTED

Simple stocking/stockinette stitch fabric but stripes are knitted in, using the intarsia method

Size:

Bag is 36cm wide x 24cm high x 4cm deep (14in x 9½in x 1½in)

How much yarn:

*3 x 50g (2oz) balls of Rowan Kid Classic, approx 140m (153 yards) per ball, in main colour M
1 ball in contrasting colour C*

Needles:

Pair of 5mm (no. 6/US 8) knitting needles

Additional items:

*Open-ended zip fastener to fit opening
Buckle to fit strap 4cm (1½in) wide
2.5m (2¾ yards) of grosgrain ribbon 4cm (1½in) wide*

Tension/gauge:

*19 sts and 25 rows measure 10cm (4in) square over st st on 5mm (no. 6/US 8) needles before felting
25 sts and 33 rows measure 10cm (4in) square over st st on 5mm (no. 6/US 8) needles after felting
IT IS ESSENTIAL TO WORK TO THE STATED TENSION/ GAUGE TO ACHIEVE SUCCESS*

What you have to do:

Cast on with main colour and also contrast colour for vertical stripes. Work in stocking/stockinette stitch. Twisting yarns together at back of work when changing colour for vertical stripes to prevent a hole forming. Wash fabric to felt it.

The Yarn

Rowan Kid Classic is a combination of lambswool and kid mohair. Its brushed appearance, with a shorter pile than is usual for most mohairs, makes it ideal for felting. When washed, the brushed fibres matt together giving the fabric its characteristic felted appearance.

 Instructions

Abbreviations:
beg = beginning;
cm = centimetre(s);
cont = continue;
dec = decrease;
foll = following;
k = knit; **p** = purl;
rem = remain;
rep = repeat;
st(s) = stitch(es);
tog = together

THE BAG: (Worked in one piece)

With M, cast on 10 sts; using shade C, cast on 4 sts; using shade M, cast on 62 sts; using shade C, cast on 4 sts; using shade M, cast on 10 sts.

1st row: K10 shade M, k4 shade C, k62 shade M, k4 shade C, k10 shade M.

2nd row: P10 shade M, p4 shade C, p 62 shade M, p4 shade C, p10 shade M.

Rep last 2 rows 34 times more. (70 rows)

With shade C, work 5 rows st st, then work 2nd row again. Rep 1st and 2nd rows 17 times, then work 1st row again. With shade C, work 5 rows st st. (116 rows) Now rep 1st and 2nd rows 35 times. 186 rows. Cast/bind off, keeping colours as set.

STRAP FOR BUCKLE:

With M, cast on 20 sts. Beg with a k row, work 12 rows st st. With shade C, work 5 rows st st. With shade M and beg with a p row, cont in st st until strap measures 82cm (32in) from beg. Cast/bind off.

SHOULDER STRAP:

With M, cast on 20 sts. Beg with a k row, work 12 rows st st. With shade C, work 5 rows st st. With shade M and beg with a p row, cont in st st until strap measures 166cm (65in) from beg, ending with a p row.

Shape end:

Dec 1 st at each end of every row until 2 sts rem. Work 2 tog and fasten off.

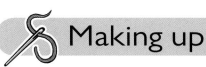
Making up

FELTING:
Place pieces in a washing machine and wash on a short cycle at 40°C (104°F) degrees. Smooth out main piece to measure about 56cm x 36cm (22in x 14in) and straps to measure 4cm (1½in) wide. Allow to dry flat.

ASSEMBLING:
Pin the grosgrain ribbon down the wrong side of one long side of both straps and catch in place with herringbone stitches. Fold straps in half with right sides facing and join long seams using backstitch. Turn straps right side out. Fold the bag in half lengthways and mark centre of base at side seams. With right sides facing, match the centre of cast-on edge of each strap to centre of base. Pin in place, then oversew the bag to the bottom of the straps and continue to join the straps to the side edges, leaving 2cm (¾in) unseamed at top. Pin zip into opening and backstitch in place. Wrap the end of the buckle strap through the buckle and stitch securely. Slot the shoulder strap through buckle, adjust and stitch in place.

HOW TO
JOIN YARN VERTICALLY

1 Knit the row in the first colour until instructed to change to the next colour. Put the right-hand needle into the stitch on the left-hand needle and then loop the new colour around the needle and make the next stitch with the new yarn.

2 At the back of the work, wind the original yarn around the new yarn and keep it tensioned with the fingers of the left hand as you continue knitting using the new yarn.

3 You repeat the same winding procedure when you want to join in the next colour. The technique is the same when working purl rows. Here you can see the white yarn wrapped around the blue yarn before the first white stitch is made.

Rib sweater with lacy panel

This tunic-style sweater is soft, flattering and easy to wear.

Make this lovely sweater with a slightly scooped neckline and raglan sleeves in a silky-feel double knitting (light worsted) yarn. It has an openwork, lacy lower panel that becomes a rib pattern as the work progresses.

The Yarn
Sirdar Flirt DK is a blend of 80% bamboo-sourced viscose and 20% wool. It produces a fabric with a soft feel and matt sheen that can be machine washed. There is a good range of contemporary colours to choose from.

GETTING STARTED

Rib pattern is fairly easy but the lacy panel might be a challenge to novices

Size:
To fit bust: 81–86[91–97:102–107]cm/32–34[36–38:40–42]in
Actual size: 92[102:111]cm/36[40:43¾]in
Length: 64[65:66]cm/25[25½:26]in
Sleeve seam: 33[34:35]cm/13[13½:13¾]in
Note: Figures in square brackets [ ] refer to larger sizes; where there is only one set of figures, it applies to all sizes

How much yarn:
13[15:16] x 50g (2oz) balls of Sirdar Flirt DK, approx 95m (104 yards) per ball

Needles:
Pair of 3.25mm (no. 10/US 3) knitting needles
Pair of 4mm (no. 8/US 6/US 6) knitting needles

Tension/gauge:
25 sts and 35 rows, when slightly stretched, measure 10cm (4in) square over rib patt on 4mm (no. 8/US 6) needles
IT IS ESSENTIAL TO WORK TO THE STATED TENSION/GAUGE TO ACHIEVE SUCCESS

What you have to do:
Work lower panel in two lacy patterns, starting with one pattern and decreasing as instructed. Work top section in rib pattern, shaping raglan armholes and neckline as instructed. Pick up stitches around neckline and knit a few rows.

Instructions

Abbreviations:

beg = beginning; **cm** = centimetre(s);
cont = continue; **dec** = decrease;
foll = follow(s)(ing); **inc** = increasing;
k = knit; **p** = purl; **patt** = pattern;
psso = pass slipped stitch over; **pwise** = purlwise;
rem = remaining; **rep** = repeat;
RS = right side; **sl** = slip; **st(s)** = stitch(es);
tog = together; **WS** = wrong side;
yfwd = yarn forward/yarn over to make a stitch;
ytb = yarn to back; **ytf** = yarn to front

BACK:

With 4mm (no. 8/US 6) needles cast on 155[171:187] sts.
K 1 row. Cont in lace patt A as foll:
1st row: (RS) K2, (yfwd, k2, sl 1, k2tog, psso, k2, yfwd, k1)
to last st, k1.
2nd row: P to end.
Rep these 2 rows to form lace patt A until work measures
19cm (7½in) from beg, ending with a RS row.
Dec row: (WS) P3, (p2tog, p1, p2tog, p3) to end.
117[129:141] sts. Cont in lace patt B as foll:
1st row: (RS) K2, (yfwd, k1, sl 1, k2tog, psso, k1, yfwd, k1)
to last st, k1.
2nd row: P to end.

Rep these 2 rows to form lace
patt B until work measures 32cm
(12½in) from beg, ending with a RS
row.
Next row: (WS) K1, (p1, k2) to
last 2 sts, p1, k1.
Cont in rib patt as foll:
1st row: (RS) P1, (ytb, sl 1 pwise,
ytf, p2) to last 2 sts, ytb, sl 1 pwise,
ytf, p1.
2nd row: K1, (p1, k2) to last 2 sts,
p1, k1. Rep these 2 rows to form
rib patt until work measures 42cm
(16½in) from beg, ending with a
WS row.
Shape raglan armholes:
Keeping patt correct, cast/bind off
4[5:6] sts at beg of next 2 rows.
109[119:129] sts.
Next row: (RS) K1, sl 1, k1, psso, patt to last 3 sts, k2tog,
k1.
Next row: P2, patt to last 2 sts, p2.
Next row: K2, patt to last 2 sts, k2.
Next row: P2, patt to last 2 sts, p2.
Rep last 4 rows 11[12:13] times more. 85[93:101] sts.*
Next row: K1, sl 1, k1, psso, patt to last 3 sts, k2tog, k1.
Next row: P2, patt to last 2 sts, p2.
Rep last 2 rows 13 times more. 57[65:73] sts. Cut off
yarn and leave rem sts on a st holder.

FRONT:

Work as given for Back to *.
Shape neck:
Next row: (RS) K1, sl 1, k1, psso, patt 25 sts, k2tog, turn
and cont on these 28 sts for left front neck.
Next row: Patt to last 2 sts, p2.
Next row: K1, sl 1, k1, psso, patt to last 2 sts, work2tog.
Rep last 2 rows 11 times more, ending with a WS row. 4 sts.
Next row: K1, sl 1, k2tog, psso. 2 sts.
Next row: P2.
K2tog and fasten off. Return to sts on holder. With RS of
work facing, sl centre 25[33:41] sts on to a holder, join
yarn to next st, work2tog, patt to last 3 sts, k2tog, k1.
Complete to match first side of neck, reversing shapings.

SLEEVES:

With 3.25mm (no. 10/US 3) needles cast on 63[69:75] sts. K 4 rows.

Change to 4mm (no. 8/US 6) needles. Cont in rib patt as foll:

1st row: (RS) P1, (ytb, sl 1 pwise, ytf, p2) to last 2 sts, ytb, sl 1 pwise, ytf, p1.

2nd row: K1, (p1, k2) to last 2 sts, p1, k1.

These 2 rows form rib patt. Cont in patt, inc 1 st at each end of next and every foll 8th row, working extra sts into patt, until there are 87[93:99] sts.

Cont straight until work measures 33[34:35] cm/13[13½:13¾]in from beg, ending with a WS row.

Shape raglan top:

Keeping patt correct, cast/bind off 4[5:6] sts at beg of next 2 rows. 79[83:87] sts.

Next row: (RS) K1, sl 1, k1, psso, patt to last 3 sts, k2tog, k1.

Next row: P2, patt to last 2 sts, p2.

Next row: K2, patt to last 2 sts, k2.

Next row: P2, patt to last 2 sts, p2.

Rep last 4 rows 3 times more. 71[75:79] sts.

Next row: K1, sl 1, k1, psso, patt to last 3 sts, k2tog, k1.

Next row: P2, patt to last 2 sts, p2.

Rep last 2 rows 29[31:33] times more. 11 sts. Cut off yarn and leave rem sts on a st holder.

NECK EDGING:

Join front and right back raglan seams.

With 3.25mm (no. 10/US 3) needles and RS facing, pick up and k across 11 sts from left sleeve, pick up and k 21 sts down left front neck, k across 25[33:41] centre front sts, pick up and k 21 sts up right front neck, k across 11 sts from right sleeve and 57[65:73] back neck sts. 146[162:178] sts. K 2 rows. Cast/bind off firmly.

Making up

Join left back raglan and edging seams. Join side and sleeve seams.

Classic beret

Give a contemporary twist to a design classic by knitting this beret in vivid colours.

Back in fashion, this easy-to-wear beret is worked flat and shaped into a circle during the knitting process. The ribbed edge has a narrow stripe in a contrasting colour.

GETTING STARTED

Fairly large number of stitches, but main fabric is simple stocking/stockinette stitch and shaping is easy

Size:
To fit an average size woman's head

How much yarn:
1 x 50g (2oz) ball of Patons Diploma Gold 4-ply, approx 184m (201 yards) per ball, in main colour M
1 ball in contrast colour C

Needles:
Pair of 2.75mm (no. 12/US 2) knitting needles
Pair of 3.25mm (no. 10/US 3) knitting needles

Tension/gauge:
28 sts and 36 rows measure 10cm (4in) square over st st on 3.25mm (no. 10/US 3) needles
IT IS ESSENTIAL TO WORK TO THE STATED TENSION/GAUGE TO ACHIEVE SUCCESS

What you have to do:
Work single rib in a contrast colour. Use main colour to work in stocking/stockinette stitch. Decrease by knitting two stitches together at regular intervals on shaping rows. Finish off by cutting yarn and threading through small number of remaining stitches.

The Yarn
Patons Diploma Gold 4-ply is a hard-wearing mixture of 55% wool, 25% acrylic and 20% nylon. It is ideal for headwear as it can be machine washed when necessary. You can choose from a large shade range of classic and contemporary colours.

Abbreviations:

alt = alternate;

beg = beginning;

cm = centimetre(s);

cont = continue;

foll = follow(s)(ing);

k = knit;

m1 = make one stitch by picking up strand lying between needles and working into back of it;

p = purl;

rem = remain;

rep = repeat;

RS = right side;

st(s) = stitch(es);

st st = stocking/stockinette stitch;

tog = together;

WS = wrong side

Instructions

BERET:

With 2.75mm (no. 12/US 2) needles and C, cast on 151 sts.

1st rib row: (RS) K1, *p1, k1, rep from * to end.

2nd rib row: P1, *k1, p1, rep from * to end. These 2 rows form rib. Cut off C. Join in M. Work a further 9 rows in rib, ending with a RS row.

Next row: (WS) Rib 2, m1, *(rib 3, m1, rib 4, m1) twice, rib 4, m1, rep from * to last 5 sts, rib 3, m1, rib 2. 193 sts.

Change to 3.25mm (no. 10/US 3) needles. Beg with a k row, cont in st st and work 36 rows, ending with a WS row.

Shape crown:

1st row: (RS) K1, *k2tog, k14, rep from * to end. 181 sts.

Work 3 rows.

5th row: K1, *k2tog, k13, rep from * to end. 169 sts.

Work 3 rows.

9th row: K1, *k2tog, k12, rep from * to end. 157 sts.

Work 3 rows. Cont in this way working 1 st less between each decrease, dec 12 sts on next and every foll 4th row until 109 sts rem. Work 1 row, so ending with a WS row.

Next row: K1, *k2tog, k7, rep from * to end. 97 sts.

Work 1 row.

Next row: K1, *k2tog, k6, rep from * to end. 85 sts.

Cont in this way working 1 st less between each decrease on every foll alt row until 13 sts rem. Cut off yarn, leaving a long end. Thread cut end of yarn through rem sts, draw up tightly and fasten off securely.

STALK:

With 3.25mm (no. 10/US 3) needles and 2 strands of C,
cast on 7 sts.
Cast/bind off knitways.

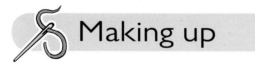 # Making up

Use long end of yarn to join seam with backstitch. Cut
a circle, approximately 30cm (12in) in diameter, from
white card. Stretch beret over card and cover with a
slightly damp cloth. Leave to dry flat, then remove card.
Sew stalk to centre of crown.

Flower power cushion

A hippy-style flower is knitted across bands of bright colours to make this stylish cushion/pillow.

For interior style reminiscent of the swinging Sixties, use the intarsia technique to make this bright striped cushion/pillow with a simple floral motif.

The Yarn

Debbie Bliss Rialto DK is 100% Merino wool that looks good when knitted in stocking/stockinette stitch. If it is carefully washed by hand when necessary, it will retain its good looks for a long time.

GETTING STARTED

The stitches are simple, but pattern is worked from a chart, using the intarsia technique of separate balls of yarn for different areas of colour across a row

Size:
Cushion/pillow is 41cm (16in) square

How much yarn:
1 x 50g (2oz) ball of Debbie Bliss Rialto DK, approx 105m (115 yards) per ball, in each of A, B, D and E
2 balls in C
Scraps of F

Needles:
Pair of 4mm (no. 8/US 6) knitting needles

Additional items:
4 flat white buttons, 2cm (¾in) in diameter
41cm (16in) square cushion pad/pillow form

Tension/gauge:
22 sts and 30 rows measure 10cm (4in) square over st st using 4mm (no. 8/US 6) needles
IT IS ESSENTIAL TO WORK TO THE STATED TENSION/GAUGE TO ACHIEVE SUCCESS

What you have to do:
Work in stocking/stockinette stitch. Read chart to work pattern. Use intarsia technique of colour knitting to work with several small balls of yarn across a row. Cast/bind off and cast on stitches to make buttonholes.

Instructions

Abbreviations:
beg = beginning; **cm** = centimetre(s);
cont = continue(ing); **k** = knit; **p** = purl;
patt = pattern; **rep** = repeat; **RS** = right side;
st(s) = stitch(es); **st st** = stocking/stockinette stitch;
WS = wrong side

FRONT:

With A, cast on 91 sts. Beg with a k row, cont in st st and patt from chart. Read odd-numbered (RS) rows from right to left and even-numbered (WS) rows from left to right. Use a separate small ball or length of yarn for each area of colour, twisting yarns together on WS of work when changing colour to avoid a hole forming. After 124th row of chart has been completed, cast/bind off.

LOWER BACK:

With 4mm (no. 8/US 6) needles and A, cast on 91 sts. Beg and ending with a k row, work 31 rows in st st. Cut off A and join in B. Beg and ending with a p row, work a further 31 rows in st st.

Cut off B and join in C.

Beg with a k row, work a further 28 rows in st st, ending with a p row.

Next row: (RS) K1, *p1, k1, rep from * to end.

Next row: P1, *k1, p1, rep from * to end. Cast/bind off in rib.

UPPER BACK:

With D, cast on 91 sts. Beg and ending with a k row, work 31 rows in st st.

Cut off D and join in C.

Beg and ending with a p row, work a further 27 rows in st st.

1st buttonhole row: (RS) K11, cast/bind off 3 sts, (k19 including st used to cast/bind off, cast/bind off 3 sts) 3 times, k to end.

2nd buttonhole row: P to end, casting on 3 sts over those cast/bound off on previous row.

Work 2 rows in k1, p1 rib as given for Lower back. Cast/bind off in rib.

Tip: To neatly sew in the ends on the front of the cushion/pillow, weave in yarn by working through the back of a few stitches on the wrong side of the work. Always work through stitches in the same colour and snip off loose ends close to the work.

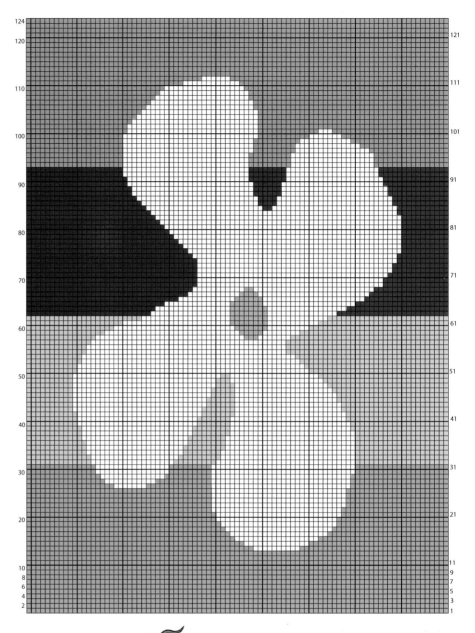

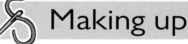 Making up

Carefully sew in all loose ends on front of cushion/pillow (see Tip). Press carefully on RS of work, using a warm iron over a dry cloth. With RS uppermost, place upper back over lower back, overlapping stripe in C at centre. Slip stitch overlapped section together along side edges. Place completed back and front together, with RS facing, and backstitch around all four sides. Turn to the right side through the centre back opening. Sew on buttons to correspond with buttonholes. Insert cushion pad/pillow form.

HOW TO
WORK IN COLOUR

The intarsia method is a way of knitting blocks of colour within a knitted fabric. A separate length of yarn is kept for each colour and the yarns are twisted together where the colours change to make a single piece of fabric without holes between the colours.

1 Instead of having a whole ball of yarn attached to each block of colour you can wind a smaller amount of yarn around a bobbin, or make a smaller ball. Plastic bobbins are available from most knitting suppliers and you simply wrap the yarn around them, working from the cut end of the yarn towards the end attached to the knitting. If you want to wind your own smaller balls, start by spreading out the finger and thumb of one hand and wrapping the yarn around them in a figure-of-eight. Remove the yarn from your fingers, keeping the shape, and then wrap the remaining yarn around the middle of the figure-of-eight. Pull the loose end from the centre of the yarn and work from this.

2 When you change to a new colour you need to twist the yarns together at the back of the work. To do this, place the new yarn over the working yarn and then wrap the new yarn around the working yarn. Pick up the new yarn and release the working yarn and continue the next stitch with the new yarn. Wrapping the new yarn around the working yarn in this way joins the two colours together vertically and stops a gap from forming between the two colours.

Striped sweater

With a simple shape and a great colour combination for the stripes, this sweater will always look crisp and fresh.

Worked in stocking/stockinette stitch and a two-colour stripe pattern, this classic fitted sweater has a nautical feel. With a scoop neck and set-in sleeves, it looks good worn casually or under a jacket for work.

GETTING STARTED

 Simple to work in stocking/stockinette stitch with basic shaping

Size:

To fit bust: 81[86:91:97]cm/32[34:36:38]in

Actual size: 90[96:100:106]cm/35½[37¾:39½:41¾]in

Length to back neck: 54[55:56:57cm/21¼[21¾:22: 22½]in

Sleeve seam: 42cm (16½in)

Note: Figures in square brackets [ ] refer to larger sizes; where there is only one set of figures, it applies to all sizes

How much yarn:

3[4:4:5] x 50g (2oz) balls of Sirdar Luxury Soft Cotton DK, approx 95m (104 yards) in colour A

4[5:6:6] balls in colour B

Needles:

Pair of 3.75mm (no. 9/US 5) knitting needles

Pair of 4mm (no. 8/US 6) knitting needles

Tension/gauge:

22 sts and 28 rows measure 10cm (4in) square over st st on 4mm (no. 8/US 6) needles

IT IS ESSENTIAL TO WORK TO THE STATED TENSION/ GAUGE TO ACHIEVE SUCCESS

What you have to do:

Work in stocking/stockinette stitch. Follow stripe pattern, carrying colour not in use up side of work. Work simple decreases and increases to shape sweater. Pick up and knit stitches around neck to work edging.

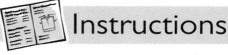 Instructions

The Yarn

Sirdar Luxury Soft Cotton DK is 100% cotton with a light twist and subtle sheen. The shade range contains beautiful fashion colours that are perfect for colour work and stripes.

STRIPE PATT:

1st–4th rows: Work 4 rows in A.

5th–10th rows: Work 6 rows in B.

11th and 12th rows: Work 2 rows in A.

13th–16th rows: Work 4 rows in B.

17th and 18th rows: Work 2 rows in A.

19th and 20th rows: Work 2 rows in B.

20th and 21st rows: Work 2 rows in A.

23rd–26th rows: Work 4 rows in B.

Rep these 26 rows to form patt.

BACK:

With 4mm (no. 8/US 6) needles and A, cast on 90[96:100:106] sts. K1 row. Beg with a k row, cont in st st

Abbreviations:

alt = alternate;
beg = beginning;
cm = centimetre(s);
cont = continue;
dec = decrease;
foll = follow(s)(ing);
inc = increase; **k** = knit;
patt = pattern;
rem = remaining;
rep = repeat;
RS = right side;
st(s) = stitch(es);
st st = stocking/stockinette stitch;
WS = wrong side

and stripe patt, AT SAME TIME shape sides by dec 1 st (2 sts in from edge) at each end of 7th and every foll 10th row to 82[88:92:98] sts. Work 11 rows straight, then inc 1 st (2 sts in from edge) at each end of next and every foll 10th row to 90[96:100:106] sts. Cont straight until work measures about 33cm (13in) from beg, ending on WS with 14th row of patt.

Shape armholes:

Keeping patt correct, cast/bind off 3 sts at beg of next 2 rows. Dec 1 st at each end of every row to 74[76:80:82] sts, then at each end of every foll alt row to 66[68:70:72] sts.*

Work straight until armholes measure 19[20:21:22]cm/ 7½[8:8¼:8¾]in from beg, ending with a WS row.

Shape shoulders and back neck:

Cast/bind off 5 sts at beg of next 2 rows. 56[58:60:62] sts.

Next row: Cast/bind off 5 sts, k18 (including st on needle after cast/

bind-off), turn and complete this side of neck first.

Cast/bind off 6 sts at beg of next 2 rows. Cast/bind off rem 6 sts.

With RS of work facing, rejoin yarn to rem sts, cast/bind off centre 10[12:14:16] sts loosely, k to end. Cast/bind off 5 sts at beg of next row, then complete to match first side of neck.

FRONT:

Work as given for Back to *. Cont straight until armholes measure 9[10:11:12]cm/ 3½[4:4½:4¾]in from beg, ending with a WS row.

Shape neck:

Next row: K27[28:29:30], turn and leave rem sts on a spare needle.

Complete this side of neck first. Keeping armhole edge straight, dec 1 st at neck edge on next 4[6:8:10] rows, then on every foll alt row to 16 sts. Work a few rows straight until Front matches Back to shoulder, ending at armhole edge.

Shape shoulder:

Cast/bind off 5 sts at beg of next and foll alt row.

Work 1 row. Cast/bind off rem 6 sts.

With RS of work facing, rejoin yarn to rem sts, cast/bind off centre 12 sts loosely, k to end. Complete to match first side of neck, reversing shaping.

SLEEVES:

With 4mm (no. 8/US 6) needles and A, cast on 46[48:50:52] sts. K1 row. Beg with a k row, cont in st st and stripe patt, inc 1 st (2 sts in from edge) at each end of 9th row and 2 foll 12th rows. Cont to inc at each end of every foll 14th row to 62[64:66:68] sts. Work straight until Sleeve measures about 42cm (16½in) from beg, ending with same patt row as Back at armholes.

Shape top:

Cast/bind off 3 sts at beg of next 2 rows. Dec 1 st at each end of next and every foll 4th row to 46[46:46:48] sts, then at each end of every foll alt row to 34[34:38:38] sts. Dec 1 st at each end of every row to 20 sts.
Cast/bind off evenly.

 Making up

Press lightly on WS according to directions on ball band. Join right shoulder seam.

Neck edging:

With 3.75mm (no. 9/US 5) needles, A and RS of work facing, pick up and k68[72:74:76] sts evenly around front neck and 32[34:36:38] sts around back neck. 100[106:110:114] sts. K 2 rows. Cast/bind off evenly.
Join left shoulder and neck edging seam.
Sew in sleeves. Join side and sleeve seams.

Envelope clutch bag

Use your knitting skills to make this pretty bag – with your choice of yarn and lining fabric, it will be unique.

Perfect for daily use, this pretty bag in a soft brushed yarn is worked in an easy textured rib pattern. Tuck it under your arm as a clutch purse, or attach a cord and use over your shoulder to keep your hands free.

GETTING STARTED

 *Bag is a simple shape and stitch pattern but care must be taken with finishing touches for a neat appearance*

Size:
Bag is 25cm wide x 12cm tall (10in x 4¾in)

How much yarn:
1 x 50g (2oz) ball of Orkney Angora 'St Magnus' 50/50 DK, approx 200m (219 yards) per ball

Needles:
Pair of 3.75mm (no. 9/US 5) knitting needles

Additional items:
1 decorative button, about 2cm (¾in) in diameter
1m (1 yard) antique gold cord
Lining fabric in co-ordinating colour
Matching sewing thread
Card for stiffening

Tension/gauge:
21 sts and 32 rows measure 10cm (4in) square over patt on 3.75mm (no. 9/US 5) needles
IT IS ESSENTIAL TO WORK TO THE STATED TENSION/GAUGE TO ACHIEVE SUCCESS

What you have to do:
Work in moss/seed stitch. Work in broken rib pattern. Shape flap by casting/binding off stitches at start of rows. Pick up and knit stitches along flap edge. Sew simple fabric lining.

The Yarn
'St Magnus' 50/50 DK from Orkney Angora is a versatile blend of lambswool with angora that exhibits all the best qualities of both fibres. There are 35 colours to choose from so it is easy to accessorize all your outfits.

Abbreviations:
beg = beginning;
cm = centimetre(s);
cont = continue;
foll = follows; **k** = knit;
p = purl; **patt** = pattern;
rep = repeat;
RS = right side;
st(s) = stitch(es);
WS = wrong side

Instructions

BAG:
Cast on 55 sts.
Next row: K1, *p1, k1, rep from *
to end.
Rep this row 5 times more to form moss/
seed st. Cont in broken rib patt as foll:
Next row: (RS) K to end.
Next row: P1, *k1, p1, rep from * to end.
Rep last 2 rows until work measures 26cm
(10¼in) from beg, ending with a WS row.

Shape flap:
Next row: Cast/bind off 3 sts knitwise,
k to end.
Next row: Cast/bind off 3 sts purlwise,
patt to end.
Rep these 2 rows 8 times more. Fasten off
last st.
Flap edging:
With RS of work facing, pick up and k59 sts
along shaped edges of flap.

BROKEN RIB
This is the main stitch used to make the bag. It makes a textured rib pattern with columns of flat knit stitch interspersed with recessed columns of purl stitches with a twisted effect.

1 The pattern is worked over two rows. Knit the first and every alternate row.

2 Begin the second row with a purl stitch and then work a knit one, purl one sequence to the end of the row.

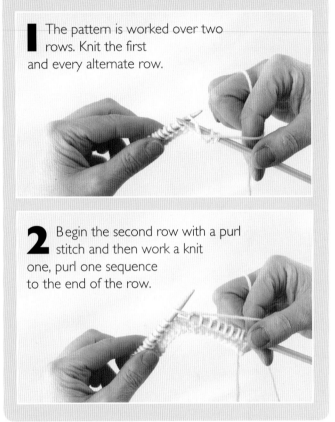

Next row: P1, *k1, p1, rep from * to end.
Cast/bind off.

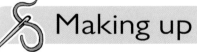

Making up

Press lightly using a warm iron over a dry cloth.
Using knitted piece as a template, cut out lining fabric, allowing 5mm (¼in) seam allowance all round. Fold seam allowance to WS and press in place.
Fold knitted piece, with RS together, so that cast-on edge is 2cm (¾in) below the flap and join side seams. Turn right side out. Make up lining fabric in the same way but leave WS out. Cut a piece of card to fit inside back of bag. Place lining in bag, then slide card in place between bag and lining. Slip stitch lining neatly in place all around opening and flap.
Make a button loop with 20cm (8in) of cord. Make a loop in the centre and secure with a knot. Tie the ends into a bow. Sew the button to the bag front, just below point of flap. Sew the cord bow to the

flap so that loop fits neatly over the button.
Measure rest of cord to required length for strap, allowing 10cm (4in) extra at each end. Make a loop at each end and tie securely. Sew a loop to the top of each side seam.

Candyfloss scarf

Practise your openwork stitch with this easy-to-knit scarf that's light as a feather.

This soft and pretty scarf is perfect to tuck in the neck of a jacket. Extra-large needles and fine brushed yarn combine to give a frothy concoction with openwork stitch panels and broken rib borders.

GETTING STARTED

 Straight piece of knitting with easy lace pattern and simple broken rib

Size:
Scarf is 18cm wide x 112cm long (7in x 44in)

How much yarn:
2 x 25g (1oz) balls of Sublime Kid Mohair, approx 112m (122 yards) per ball

Needles:
Pair of 6mm (no. 4/US 10) knitting needles

Tension/gauge:
16 sts and 20 rows measure 10cm (4in) square over broken rib patt on 6mm (no. 4/US 10) needles
IT IS ESSENTIAL TO WORK TO THE STATED TENSION/GAUGE TO ACHIEVE SUCCESS

What you have to do:
Work in broken rib pattern by knitting one row, then working one row in single rib. Work simple decorative increases and decreases for lace pattern.

The Yarn
Sublime Kid Mohair is a luxurious yarn spun from 60% of the very softest quality of kid mohair blended with 35% nylon and a 5% touch of merino wool. It is amazingly light and comes in eight misty, feminine colours.

 # Instructions

Abbreviations:

cm = centimetre(s); **cont**
= continue;
foll = following; **k** = knit;
p = purl; **rep** = repeat;
RS = right side;
st(s) = stitch(es);
tog = together;
WS = wrong side;
yo = yarn over needle to
make a decorative increase

SCARF:

Cast on 29 sts.

Work rib patt for edging as foll:

1st row: (WS) K1, *p1, k1, rep from * to end.
2nd row: K to end.

Rep these 2 rows 3 times more, then work 1st row again.

Cont in lace patt with ribbed edges as foll:

1st row: (RS) K to end.
2nd row: (K1, p1) twice, k1, *yo, k2tog, rep from * to last 6 sts, k2, (p1, k1) twice.
3rd row: K to end.
4th row: (K1, p1) twice, k2, *yo, k2tog, rep from * to last 5 sts, k1, (p1, k1) twice.

Rep these 4 rows 5 times more (24 rows in total).

Work rib patt as foll:

1st row: (RS) K to end.
2nd row: K1, *p1, k1, rep from * to end.

Rep these 2 rows 4 times more (10 rows in total).

Alternating lace and rib patts, rep them 4 times more, then work 24 rows in lace patt, until Scarf measures approximately 108cm (42½in), ending with a WS row.

Work 8 rows in rib patt for edging. Cast/bind off knitwise.

 # Making up

Pin out to given measurements. Steam gently to straighten side edges and raise the pile.

HOW TO
CREATE THE OPENWORK STITCH

Mohair yarn worked with large needles creates large airy stitches that show off the fine-spun yarn to its best advantage.

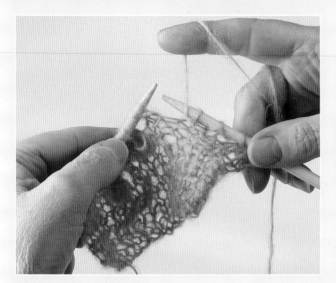

I The openwork stitch is created by a combination of yarn-over increases and knit-two-together decreases. Begin the second row of the lace pattern by working the broken rib edge, then knit one. Bring the yarn to the front of the work and take it over the right-hand needle to the back to create a yarn-over increase (yo).

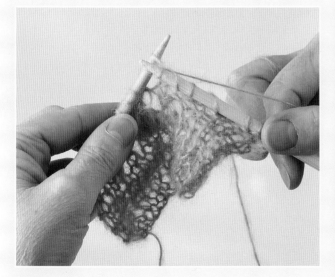

2 Knit the next two stitches together to decrease a stitch. Continue with this yarn-over, knit-two-together sequence to the last six stitches. Knit two and then work the broken rib edge.

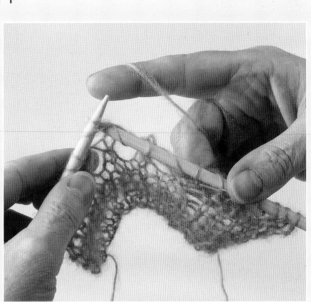

3 Working each wrong-side row with yarn-over increases and knit-two-together decreases, and then knitting each right-side row creates a pattern of interlinked 'holes' and gives the lacy effect to this openwork stitch.

Romantic cushion

Make this cushion/pillow for a romantic gift or to complete your décor with a pink accent.

This stocking-stitch cushion/pillow has a pretty ribbon and bead-trimmed heart stitched onto the front.

GETTING STARTED

Cover and heart are both in basic stocking/stockinette stitch fabric, but heart requires some simple shaping

Size:
Cushion/pillow is 38cm x 38cm (15in x 15in)

How much yarn:
*4 x 50g (2oz) balls of Debbie Bliss Cashmerino DK, approx 110m (120 yards) per ball, in main colour A
1 x 50g (2oz) ball of Debbie Bliss Cathay, approx 100m (110 yards) per ball, in contrast colour B*

Needles:
*Pair of 3.75mm (no. 9/US 5) knitting needles
Pair of 4mm (no. 8/US 6) knitting needles*

Additional items:
*Approximately 100 medium-sized beads
1m (40in) of organza ribbon 1.5cm (⅝in) wide
Sewing needle and matching thread for sewing on beads
38cm (15in) square cushion pad/pillow form*

Tension/gauge:
*With yarn A, 22 sts and 30 rows measure 10cm (4in) square over st st on 4mm (no. 8/US 6) needles; with yarn B, 22 sts and 30 rows measure 10cm (4in) square over st st on 3.75mm (no. 9/US 5) needles
IT IS ESSENTIAL TO WORK TO THE STATED TENSION/GAUGE TO ACHIEVE SUCCESS*

What you have to do:
Work two square pieces of stocking/stockinette stitch for cushion/pillow cover. Work heart in stocking/stockinette stitch in a different yarn. Make simple increases and decreases to form heart shape. Decorate heart with ribbon and beads. Sew heart onto front.

The Yarn

Debbie Bliss Cashmerino DK for the cover is a luxurious blend of 55% merino wool with 33% microfibre and 12% cashmere. Its smooth finish and great choice of colours is ideal for stocking/stockinette-stitch fabrics. The heart is in Cathay a silky cotton blend with a rich sheen that provides a good contrast against the wool background.

Instructions

Abbreviations:
beg = beginning;
cm = centimetre(s);
cont = continue; **k** = knit;
p = purl; **psso** = pass
slipped stitch over;
rep = repeat;
RS = right side; **sl** = slip;
st(s) = stitch(es);
st st = stocking/stockinette
stitch;
tbl = through back of
loops;
tog = together

FRONT:
With 4mm (no. 8/US 6) needles and A, cast on 81 sts. Beg with a k row, cont in st st until work measures 38cm (15in) from beg, ending with a p row. Cast/bind off.

BACK:
Work as given for Front.

HEART:
First side:
With 3.75mm (no. 9/US 5) needles and B, cast on 8 sts and work from top of heart down. P 1 row. K 1 row and p 1 row, cast on 3 sts at beg of each row. 14 sts.
Next row: (K1, k1 tbl) into next st, k to last 2 sts, (k1, k1 tbl) into next st, k1.
Next row: (P1, p1 tbl) into next st, p to last 2 sts, (p1, p1 tbl) into next st, p1.
Rep last 2 rows once, then work first of them again. 24 sts. P 1 row.
Next row: (K1, k1 tbl) into next st, k to last 2 sts,

(k1, k1 tbl) into next st, k1. 26 sts. Work 3 rows in st st.**
Cut off yarn and leave these sts on the needle.

Second side:
With other 3.75mm (no. 9/US 5) needle and B, cast on 8 sts and work as given for first side to **.

Join pieces:
Next row: (K1, k1 tbl) into next st, k24, (k1, k1 tbl) into next st, then with RS facing, k across 24 sts of first side, (k1, k1 tbl) into next st, k1. 55 sts.
Work 17 rows in st st, ending with a p row.
Next row: K2tog tbl, k to last 2 sts, k2tog.
Work 5 rows in st st.
Next row: K2tog tbl, k to last 2 sts, k2tog.
Work 3 rows in st st.
Next row: K2tog tbl, k to last 2 sts, k2tog.
P 1 row. Rep last 2 rows to 29 sts, ending with a k row.
Next row: P2tog, p to last 2 sts, p2tog tbl.
Next row: K2tog tbl, k to last 2 sts, k2tog.
Rep last 2 rows to 3 sts, ending with a p row.
Next row: Sl 1, k2tog, psso. Fasten off.

HOW TO
WORK SIMPLE DECREASES

The heart element is shaped in various ways. To increase, the shaping stitches are either cast on at the beginning of the row or some stitches are worked into twice to make an extra stitch. To decrease, stitches are either knitted together as usual or knitted together through the back of the loops. These simple decreases are shown here.

Knit two together:

1 Knit to the instructed point and then on the instruction K2tog, insert the right-hand needle into the next two stitches on the left-hand needle. Wrap the yarn around the right-hand needle in the usual way and complete the stitch.

 Making up

Press pieces according to directions on ball bands.

Using the photograph (left), as a guide, thread ribbon around heart, about three stitches in from the edge. Making sure it is centralized, sew heart onto cushion/pillow front with a slip stitch, using yarn B. Sew beads on to edge of heart using sewing thread and spacing them about 1cm (½in) apart. With RS facing, join front and back around three sides with backstitch. Turn RS out. Insert cushion pad/pillow form and neatly slip stitch opening closed.

2 One stitch is decreased although this is almost invisible in the completed row.

Knit two together through back of loop:

1 Work the row until the point when you are instructed to k2tog tbl. Insert the right-hand needle into the back of the loops of the first two stitches on the left-hand needle from right to left. Wrap the yarn around the right-hand needle and complete the stitch.

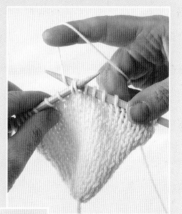

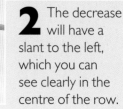

2 The decrease will have a slant to the left, which you can see clearly in the centre of the row.

Soft cable sweater

This sweater has classic elegant lines; knitted in soft angora, it's a romantic masterpiece.

Cuddle up in this timeless sweater with set-in sleeves and round neck. Knitted in the softest angora blend, it features a simple, yet stylish cable panel on the front.

GETTING STARTED

The cable panel may seem daunting, but it is formed with the simplest rope cables

Size:

To fit bust: 76–81[86–91:97–102]cm/30–32[34–36:38–40]in

Actual size: 87[95:103.5]cm/34¼[37½:40¾]in

Length: 50[53:56]cm/19¾[21:22]in

Sleeve seam: 45[46:47]cm/17¾[18:18½]in

Note: Figures in square brackets [ ] refer to larger sizes; where there is only one set of figures, it applies to all sizes

How much yarn:

4[5:6] x 50g (2oz) balls of Orkney Angora 'St Magnus' 50/50 DK, approx 200m (219 yards) per ball

Needles:

Pair of 3.75mm (no. 9/US 5) knitting needles
Pair of 4.5mm (no. 7/US 7) knitting needles
Cable needle

Additional items:

Two stitch holders

Tension/gauge:

22 sts and 28 rows measure 10cm (4in) square over st st worked on 4.5mm (no. 7/US 7) needles. Cable panel (49 sts) measures 14cm (5½in) across

IT IS ESSENTIAL TO WORK TO THE STATED TENSION/ GAUGE TO ACHIEVE SUCCESS

What you have to do:

Work welt in single (k1, p1) rib. Work back in stocking/ stockinette stitch. Work front in stocking/stockinette stitch with central cable pattern panel. Make simple rope cables. Work simple decreases and increases to shape sweater. Pick up stitches around neckline to work neckband in single rib.

The Yarn

Orkney Angora 'St Magnus' 50/50 DK is a blend of unbrushed, finest grade angora and best-quality lambswool. This soft yarn (it becomes slightly fluffy with handling, washing and wearing) is extremely versatile for accessories and garments, and is available in 35 superb shades.

 Instructions

Abbreviations:

alt = alternate;
beg = beginning;
cm = centimetre(s);
cont = continue;
C6B = slip next 3 sts on to cable needle and leave at back of work, k3, then k3 sts from cable needle;
C6F = slip next 3 sts on to cable needle and leave at front of work, k3, then k 3 sts from cable needle;
dec = decrease(ing);
foll = follow(s)(ing);
inc = increase(ing);
k = knit;
kfb = knit into front and back of stitch; **p** = purl;
patt = pattern;
pfb = purl into front and back of stitch;
psso = pass slipped stitch over;
rem = remaining;
rep = repeat;
RS = right side; **sl** = slip;
st(s) = stitch(es);
st st = stocking/stockinette stitch;
tbl = through back of loops; **tog** = together;
WS = wrong side

BACK:

With 3.75mm (no. 9/US 5) needles cast on 95[105:115] sts.
1st row: (RS) K1, *p1, k1, rep from * to end.
2nd row: P1, *k1, p1, rep from * to end.
Rep these 2 rows twice more.
Change to 4.5mm (no. 7/US 7) needles.
Beg with a k row, work 86[90:94] rows in st st, ending with a p row.

Shape armholes:

Cast/bind off 3[4:5] sts at beg of next 2 rows.
Next row: K1, sl 1, k1, psso, k to last 3 sts, k2tog, k1.
Next row: P to end.
Rep last 2 rows 4[5:6] times more, then work first of them again. 77[83:89] sts.
Work 39[41:43] rows straight, ending with a p row.

Shape shoulders:

Cast/bind off 8[9:10] sts at beg of next 4 rows. Cut off yarn. Leave rem 45[47:49] sts on a holder.

FRONT:

With 3.75mm (no. 9/US 5) needles cast on 103[111:119] sts. Rib 5 rows as given for Back.
Inc row: (WS) Rib 33[37:41], (kfb, rib 2, pfb, rib 2, kfb, rib 3) 3 times, kfb, rib 2, pfb, rib 2, kfb, rib 33[37:41]. 115[123:131] sts.
Change to 4.5mm (no. 7) needles. Work in cable panel patt as foll:
1st row: (RS) K33[37:41], (p2, k6, p2, k3) 3 times, p2, k6, p2, k33[37:41].
2nd row: P33[37:41], (k2, p6, k2, p3) 3 times, k2, p6, k2, p33[37:41].
3rd–6th rows: Rep 1st and 2nd rows twice.
7th row: K33[37:41], (p2, C6B, p2, k3) twice, p2, C6F, p2, k3, p2, C6F, p2, k33[37:41].
8th row: As 2nd row.
The last 8 rows form cable panel patt.
Patt 78[82:86] rows more, ending with a 6th[2nd:6th] patt row.

Shape armholes:

Cast/bind off 3[4:5] sts at beg of next 2 rows.
Next row: K1, sl 1, k1, psso, patt to last 3 sts, k2tog, k1.
Next row: Patt to end.
Rep last 2 rows 4[5:6] times more, then work first of them again. 97[101:105] sts.
Patt 31[33:35] rows straight, ending with a 2nd patt row.

Shape neck:

Next row: (RS) K21[23:25], k2tog, k1, turn and complete this side of neck first.
Next row: P1, p2tog, p to end.
Cont to dec 1 st at neck edge in this way on next 6 rows. 16[18:20] sts.

Shape shoulder:

Cast/bind off 8[9:10] sts at beg of next row. Work 1 row.

Cast/bind off rem 8[9:10] sts.
With RS of work facing, sl centre 49 sts on to a holder, rejoin yarn to next st, k1, sl 1, k1, psso, k to end.
Next row: P to last 3 sts, p2tog tbl, p1.
Complete as first side of neck, reversing shaping as shown and working 1 row straight before shaping shoulder.

SLEEVES: (Make 2)

With 3.75mm (no. 9/US 5) needles cast on 43[47:51] sts. Rib 6 rows as given for Back.
Change to 4.5mm (no. 7/US 7) needles. Beg with a k row, cont in st st, inc 1 st at each end of next and every foll 8th row to 71[77:83] sts. Work 15[11:5] rows straight, ending with a p row.

Shape sleeve top:

Cast/bind off 3[4:5] sts at beg of next 2 rows. Dec 1 st at each end of next and every foll alt row to 39[41:43] sts, then at each end of every row to 21[23:25] sts. Cast/bind off 3 sts at beg of next 4 rows. Cast/bind off rem 9[11:13] sts.

NECKBAND:

Join right shoulder seam.
With 3.75mm (no. 9/US 5) needles and RS of work facing, pick up and k9 sts down left front neck, k across sts on holder as foll: (p2tog, k2, k2tog, k2, p2tog, k3) 3 times, p2tog, k2, k2tog, k2, p2tog, pick up and k9 sts up right front neck, k across 45[47:49] back neck sts. 100[102:104] sts.
Work 5 rows in k1, p1 rib. Cast/bind off in rib.

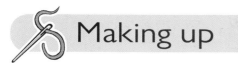 Making up

Do not press. Join left shoulder and neckband seam. Sew in sleeves. Join side and sleeve seams.

Op-art throw

Create an optical illusion with this black-and-white throw based on a design of squares within squares.

The striking combination of black and white with the colours reversed in alternate squares makes a graphic pattern for this contemporary throw. Worked in stocking/stockinette stitch, it has a striped garter-stitch edging.

The Yarn

Debbie Bliss Eco Aran is a beautiful Aran (fisherman) weight yarn in 100% organic cotton. The yarn is dyed with non-toxic dyes and there is a vibrant range of colours to choose from.

GETTING STARTED

Squares are in basic fabric but require knowledge of colour work techniques. Size of throw means that working edgings needs some care

Size:
Throw measures 120cm x 150cm (47in x 59in)

How much yarn:
16 x 50g (2oz) balls of Debbie Bliss Eco Aran, approx 75m (82 yards) per ball, in main colour A
15 balls in contrast colour B

Needles:
Pair of 5mm (no. 6/US 8) knitting needles
5mm (no. 6/US 8) circular knitting needle, 80cm or 100cm long (32in or 40in)

Tension/gauge:
16.5 sts and 24.5 rows measure 10cm (4in) square over chart patt on 5mm (no. 6/US 8) needles
IT IS ESSENTIAL TO WORK TO THE STATED TENSION/GAUGE TO ACHIEVE SUCCESS

What you have to do:
Make squares in stocking/stockinette stitch and two colours following a chart. Use intarsia technique for colour work (twisting yarns together on wrong side of work) for sections of each square. Make long strips of squares, then sew strips together to form throw. Pick up stitches along each side and work edging in garter stitch and stripes.

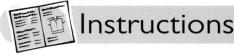 Instructions

Abbreviations:

beg = beginning; **cm** = centimetre(s); **cont** = continue; **foll** = follows; **g st** = garter stitch (every row knit); **k** = knit; **p** = purl; **patt** = pattern; **rep** = repeat; **RS** = right side; **st(s)** = stitch(es); **st st** = stocking/stockinette stitch; **tog** = together; **WS** = wrong side

THROW:

1st row, Square 1: With 5mm (no. 6/US 8) needles and A, cast on 26 sts. Beg with a k row, cont in st st and patt from chart, reading odd-numbered (k) rows from right to left and even-numbered (p) rows from left to right. Over centre 26 rows, use small separate balls of yarn for each area of colour, twisting yarns tog on WS of work when changing colour. When 38 rows have been completed, cast/bind off.

Square 2: With 5mm (no. 6/US 8) needles, B and RS of Square 1 facing, pick up and k 26 sts along cast/bound-off edge of Square 1. Work as given for Square 1, reversing the colours.

Cont in this way until there are 9 squares in 1st row. Make 6 more rows of Squares, reversing the colours each time as shown in the diagram on page 55.

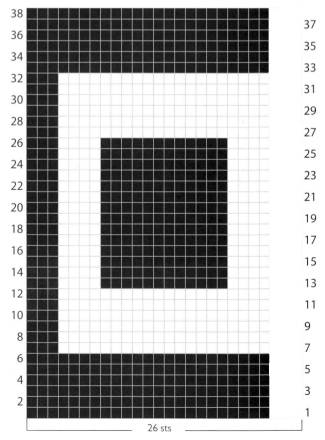

 Making up

Press rows of Squares according to directions on ball band. Using mattress stitch, join rows together as shown in diagram to form throw.

Side edgings:

With 5mm (no. 6/US 8) circular needle, A and RS of throw facing, pick up and k 172 sts along one long edge. *Working forwards and backwards in rows, k 1 row. Cont in g st and stripes as foll: (2 rows B and 2 rows A) 3 times, 2 rows B and 1 row A. Cast/bind off knitwise on WS with A. *

Rep edging on other long edge of throw.

Top and bottom edgings:

With 5mm (no. 6/US 8) circular needle, A and RS of throw facing, pick up and k 9 sts across end of side edging, then 175 sts along top edge of throw (picking up 25 sts from cast/bound-off edge of each square) and 9 sts across end of other side edging. 193 sts. Work as given for side edging from * to *.

Rep edging on bottom edge of throw.

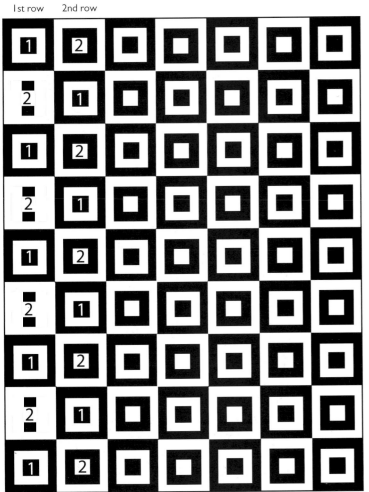

1st row   2nd row

Felted bucket bag

This bucket bag is perfect for trips around town. The shape is great and the felting process adds an interesting texture.

Worked in the round, this classic-shaped bag has no obvious seams. The flower trims add a touch of designer class.

GETTING STARTED

Basic stocking/stockinette stitch fabric but working in rounds with a circular needle may seem unfamiliar at first and felting will take some time and patience

Size:
After felting, bag is 22cm high x 34cm wide x 9cm deep (8½in x 13½in x 3½in)

How much yarn:
6 x 50g (2oz) balls of Twilleys Freedom Wool, approx 50m (55 yards) per ball, in main colour A
1 x 25g (1oz) ball of Rowan Kidsilk Haze, approx 210m (229 yards) per ball, in contrast colour B for flowers

Needles:
10mm (no. 000/US 15) circular knitting needle, 80cm (32in) long
Pair of 4mm (no. 8/US 6) knitting needles

Additional items:
Stitch markers
4 small orange buttons

Tension/gauge:
10 sts and 14 rows measure 10cm (4in) square over st st before felting on 10mm (no. 000/US 15) needles
IT IS ESSENTIAL TO WORK TO THE STATED TENSION/ GAUGE TO ACHIEVE SUCCESS

What you have to do:
Cast on for top edge of bag and join into a circle. Work in rounds of stocking/stockinette stitch (every round knit). Shape fabric with simple decreases at either side of markers. Close lower edge by grafting stitches together. Knit decorative flowers to trim ends of handles.

The Yarn
Twilleys Freedom Wool is 100% pure wool. Its loosely spun fibres produce a chunky and lightweight fabric that felts beautifully when washed in a machine. Rowan Kidsilk Haze is used for the decorative flowers.

 Instructions

Abbreviations:
cm = centimetre(s); **foll** = follows; **g st** = garter stitch (every row knit); **k** = knit; **kfb** = knit into front and back of stitch; **p** = purl; **psso** = pass slipped stitch over; **rep** = repeat; **sl** = slip; **st(s)** = stitch(es); **st st** = stocking/ stockinette stitch; **tog** = together; **yfwd** = yarn forward/ yarn over between needles

BAG:

Note: The body of the bag is worked in one piece.
With 10mm (no. 000/US 15) circular needle and
A, cast on 94 sts. Making sure that the cast-on row
is not twisted, join into a circle and work in rounds.
Place a stitch marker to denote end of round and
another after 47 sts to denote halfway point.
Cont in st st (every round knit), work 7 rounds.
Next round: (K to 2 sts before marker,
k2tog) twice.
Rep last 8 rounds 5 times more. 82 sts. Work
7 more rounds straight, placing 4 more markers
8 sts either side of previous 2 markers on last round
as foll:
Work 8 sts, shaping marker, 25 sts, shaping marker,
8 sts, halfway marker, 8 sts, shaping marker, 25 sts,
shaping marker, 8 sts, end marker.

Shape end:

Next round: K to 2 sts before each of 4 shaping
markers, sl 1, k1, psso, slip marker, k2tog.
Rep last round 6 times more. 26 sts.
Next round: (K2tog over shaping marker, k to
2 sts before marker at halfway point, sl 1, k1, psso)
twice. 22 sts.
Graft rem sts tog to close bottom edge.

HANDLES: (Make 2)

With 10mm (no. 000/US 15) circular needle and
A, cast on 6 sts. Working in rows, cont in g st until
handle measures 52cm (20½in). Cast/bind off.

FLOWERS: (Make 4)

With 4mm (no. 8/US 6) needles and B, cast on 57 sts.
1st row: P to end.
2nd row: K2, (k1, sl st back to left needle, lift next
8 sts on left needle over this st and off needle, yfwd
and k first st again, k2) 5 times. 22 sts.
3rd row: P1, (p2tog, kfb, p1) 5 times, p1. 22 sts.
4th row: K2tog to end. 11 sts.
5th row: P2tog to last st, p1, then lift 2nd, 3rd, 4th,
5th and 6th sts over first st. Fasten off.
Join seam to form a circular shape.

Making up

FELTING:
Place bag and handles (not flowers) in a pillowcase and fasten with a safety pin. Machine wash with detergent at 60°C (140°F) degrees on a short wash. Shape while wet and allow to dry.

ASSEMBLING:
Sew the ends of the handles securely to the front of the bag about 5cm (2in) below top edge. Attach a flower with a button at its centre to the end of each handle.

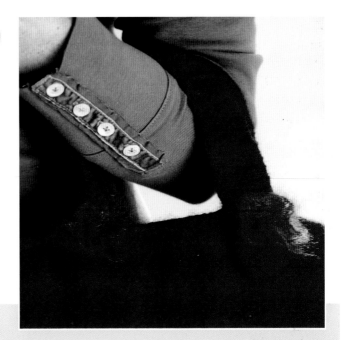

HOW TO
USE CIRCULAR NEEDLES

A circular needle is used to make a tubular piece of knitting, as you knit round in a continuous circle. You can cast on and knit whole items on circular needles or use them to pick up stitches and knit a neck or a round shape. Circular needles consist of two short straight needles joined by a flexible plastic wire. They are available in sizes just like ordinary knitting needles and they also come in several lengths; the needles and connecting wire should be short enough so the stitches are not stretched when joined.

1 Cast on or pick up stitches as you would for ordinary knitting using a regular needle. Distribute the stitches evenly around the needles and wire, making sure they all lie in the same direction and are not twisted.

3 Hold the needle with the last cast-on stitch in your right hand and the needle with the first cast-on stitch in your left hand. Knit the first cast-on stitch, keeping the yarn well tensioned to avoid a gap.

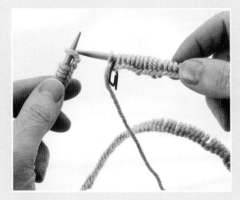

2 The last cast-on stitch is the last stitch of the round. Place a marker here to indicate the end of the round.

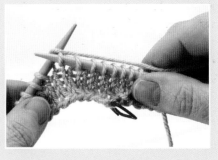

4 Work until you reach the marker, checking that the stitches are eased around the needles as you work. This completes the first round. Continue knitting in this way for the required depth of the fabric tube.

Wrap top

This ballerina-style top has been adapted and refined to make a great-looking addition to your wardrobe.

Look elegant in this classic crossover top with set-in sleeves that fastens around the waist with ties. Worked in stocking/stockinette stitch with moss/seed stitch borders, it will be a perennial favourite in your wardrobe.

GETTING STARTED

Easy to knit in stocking/stockinette stitch but pay attention to simultaneous shaping of front and side edges on the fronts

Size:

To fit bust: *81–86[91–97:102–107]cm/32–34[36–38:40–42]in*

Actual size: *88[99:110]cm/34½in[39:43½]in*

Length: *53[56:59]cm/21[22:23¼]in*

Sleeve seam: *44[45:47]cm/17½[17¾:18½]in*

Note: *Figures in square brackets [ ] refer to larger sizes; where there is only one set of figures, it applies to all sizes*

How much yarn:

10[11:11] x 50g (2oz) balls of Sublime Extra Fine Merino Wool DK, approx 116m (127 yards) per ball

Needles:

Pair of 3.25mm (no. 10/US 3) knitting needles
Pair of 4mm (no. 8/US 6) knitting needles

Tension/gauge:

22 sts and 28 rows measure 10cm (4in) square over st st on 4mm (no. 8/US 6) needles
IT IS ESSENTIAL TO WORK TO THE STATED TENSION/GAUGE TO ACHIEVE SUCCESS

What you have to do:

Work main fabric in stocking/stockinette stitch with integrated moss/seed stitch-borders. Work simple shaping for side, armhole and front edges. Make separate ties and sew on afterwards.

The Yarn

Sublime Extra Fine Merino Wool DK is 100% natural as its name implies. Spun from the finest quality of merino wool, it is a luxuriously smooth yarn giving clear stitch definition. It comes in a colour palette of 20 beautiful subtle shades.

Abbreviations:

alt = alternate;
beg = beginning;
cm = centimetre(s);
cont = continue;
dec = decrease;
foll = follow(s)(ing);
inc = increase; **k** = knit;
m1 = make one stitch by picking up horizontal strand lying between needles and working into back of it;
p = purl;
psso = pass slipped stitch over;
rem = remaining;
rep = repeat;
RS = right side; **sl** = slip;
st(s) = stitch(es);
st st = stocking/ stockinette stitch;
tbl = through back of loops;
tog = together;
WS = wrong side

Instructions

BACK:

With 3.25mm (no. 10/US 3) needles cast on 99[111:123] sts.
1st row: K1, (p1, k1) to end.
Rep this row to form moss/seed st. Work 5 rows more.
Change to 4mm (no. 8/US 6) needles.
Next row: K3, sl 1, k1, psso, k to last 5 sts, k2tog, k3.
Beg with a p row, work 5 rows in st st.
Rep last 6 rows 4[5:5] times more, then work dec row again. 87[97:109] sts. Beg with a p row, work 5[3:7] rows straight. Insert markers at each end of last row to indicate waistline.
Next row: K3, m1, k to last 3 sts, m1, k3.
Work 5[5:7] rows in st st. Rep last 6[6:8] rows 4[5:5] times more, then work inc row again. 99[111:123] sts. Work 25[21:11] rows straight, ending with a p row.

Shape armholes:

Cast/bind off 6[7:8] sts at beg of next 2 rows. 87[97:107] sts. Dec 1 st at each end of next and foll 8[10:12] alt rows. 69[75:81] sts. Work 35[33:31] rows straight, ending with a p row.

Shape shoulders:

Cast/bind off 16[18:19] sts at beg of next 2 rows.
Change to 3.25mm (no. 10/US 3) needles. Work 4 rows in moss/seed st on rem 37[39:43] sts. Cast/bind off firmly in moss/seed st.

LEFT FRONT:

With 3.25mm (no. 10/US 3) needles cast on 91[103:115] sts. Work 6 rows in moss/seed st.
Change to 4mm (no. 8/US 6) needles.
Next row: K3, sl 1, k1, psso, k to last 3 sts, work 3 sts in moss/seed st for front border.
Next row: Work 3 sts in moss/seed st, p to end.
Work 4 rows straight, keeping border as set. Rep last 6 rows 4[5:5] times more, then work dec row again. 85[96:108] sts. Work 5[3:7] rows straight, ending on WS. Insert markers at each end of last row to indicate waistline.
Next row: K3, m1, k to last 5 sts, k2tog, work 3 sts in moss/seed st.
Next row: Work 3 sts in moss/seed st, p2tog, p to end.
Work 4[4:6] rows more, keeping side edge straight and dec 1 st at front edge on every row as set. Rep last 6[6:8] rows 4[5:5] times more, then work 1st row again. 60[66:66] sts. Work 25[21:11] rows, keeping side edge straight and dec 1 st at front edge on every RS row. 48[56:61] sts.

Shape armhole:

Next row: Cast/bind off 6[7:8] sts, k to last 5 sts, k2tog, work 3 sts in moss/seed st.

Cont to dec as set at front edge, AT SAME TIME dec 1 st at armhole edge on every RS row until 23[26:26] sts rem. Keeping armhole edge straight, cont to dec at front edge only on every foll 4th row until 19[21:22] sts rem. Work 19[13:15] rows straight, ending with a WS row. Cast/bind off.

RIGHT FRONT:

With 3.25mm (no. 10/US 3) needles cast on 91[103:115] sts. Work 6 rows in moss/seed st. Change to 4mm (no. 8/US 6) needles.

Next row: Work 3 sts in moss/seed st, k to last 5 sts, k2tog, k3.

Next row: P to last 3 sts, work 3 sts in moss/seed st. Work 4 rows straight, keeping border as set. Rep last 6 rows 4[5:5] times more, then work dec row again. 85[96:108] sts. Work 5[3:7] rows straight, ending on WS. Insert markers at each end of last row to indicate waistline.

Next row: Work 3 sts in moss/seed st, sl 1, k1, psso, k to last 3 sts, m1, k3.

Next row: P to last 5 sts, p2tog tbl, work 3 sts in moss/seed st.

Work as given for Left front from * to *.

Next row: Work 3 sts in moss/seed st, sl 1, k1, psso, k to end.

Shape armhole:

Next row: Cast/bind off 6[7:8] sts, p to last 3 sts, work 3 sts in moss/seed st.

Complete as given for Left front, noting that 1 more row will be worked before casting/binding off for shoulder.

SLEEVES: (Make 2)

With 3.25mm (no. 10/US 3) needles cast on 47[49:53] sts. Work 6 rows moss/seed st.

Change to 4mm (no. 8/US 6) needles.

Next row: K3, m1, k to last 3 sts, m1, k3.

Beg with a p row, work 9 rows in st st. Rep last 10 rows 10[11:11] times more, then work inc row again. 71[75:79] sts. Work 9[3:7] rows straight, ending with a p row.

Shape top:

Cast/bind off 6[7:8] sts at beg of next 2 rows. Dec 1 st at each end of next row and foll 12[14:16] alt rows, then on every row until 15[17:19] sts rem. Cast/bind off.

TIES: (Make 2)

With 3.25mm (no. 10/US 3) needles cast on 5 sts. Work in moss st until tie measures 56cm (22in). Cast/bind off in moss/seed st.

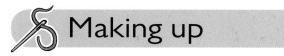

Making up

Join shoulder and neck edging seams. Sew in sleeves. Join sleeve and side seams, leaving a 2cm (¾in) gap at waistline on right side seam for tie. Sew ties to front edges at waistline.

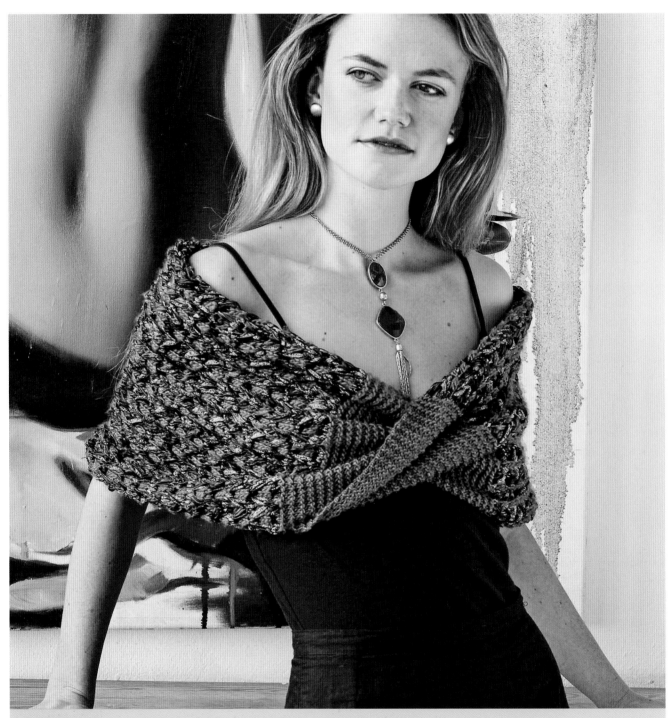

Twist wrap

This clever twist top uses ribbon yarn to great effect to create an elegant fabric with a metallic sheen.

Glamorous enough for any occasion, this wrap with a single twist at the front will not fall off your shoulders. It is knitted in two luxury yarns and a slip-stitch pattern to create a fabulous textured fabric.

GETTING STARTED

Wrap is a straight piece of fabric but pattern will need some practice first

Size:
Wrap is approximately 38cm wide x 90[96:100]cm long (15in x 35½[37¾:39½]in)

How much yarn:
4 x 50g (2oz) balls of Louisa Harding Grace, approx 100m (100 yards) per ball, in colour A
4 x 100g (3½oz) hanks of Louisa Harding Sari Ribbon, approx 120m (131) yards per hank, in colour B

Needles:
Pair of 5mm (no. 6/US 8) knitting needles
Cable needle

Additional items:
Matching sewing thread and needle

Tension/gauge:
21 sts and 25 rows measure 10cm (4in) square over patt on 5mm (no. 6/US 8) needles
IT IS ESSENTIAL TO WORK TO THE STATED TENSION/GAUGE TO ACHIEVE SUCCESS

What you have to do:
Work a slip-stitch and cable pattern using two yarns and colours. Knit a garter-stitch section in the centre. Work pattern in reverse for second half. Make a single twist in garter-stitch section before sewing ends of wrap together.

The Yarn
Louisa Harding Grace is a blend of 50% silk and 50% merino wool in a double knitting (light worsted) weight. It has a slight pearlised sheen and is available in a small range of colours. Louisa Harding Sari Ribbon is an exotic ribbon yarn containing 90% nylon and 10% metallic. There is a range of variegated colours, each containing a central strip of metallic threads.

 Instructions

WRAP: (Worked in one piece)
With 5mm (no. 6/US 8) needles and A, cast on 80 sts.
Foundation row: (RS) With B, k to end.
Now cont in patt as foll:
1st row: (WS) With B, p1, pw2, p4, *(pw2) twice, p4, rep from * to last 2 sts, pw2, p1.
2nd row: With A, k1, sl 1p allowing extra loop to fall off needle, k4, *sl 2p allowing extra loops to fall off needle, k4, rep from * to last 2 sts, sl 1p allowing extra loop to fall off needle, k1.
3rd row: With A, p1, sl 1p, p4, *sl 2p, p4, rep from * to last 2 sts, sl 1p, p1.
4th row: With A, k1, sl 1p, k4, *sl 2p, k4, rep from * to last 2 sts, sl 1p, k1.
5th row: As 3rd row.
6th row: With B, k1, *c3f, c3b, rep from * to last st, k1.
These 6 rows form patt. Cont in patt until work measures 45[48:50]cm/17¾[19:19¾]in, ending with 6th row. With B only, p 1 row.
Dec row: With A, k3, k2tog, *k4, k2tog, rep from * to last 3 sts, k3. 67 sts. Now cont in g st for 15cm (6in), ending on a WS row.
Inc row: With A, k3, k into front and back of next st,

Abbreviations:

beg = beginning;

cm = centimetre(s);

cont = continue;

c3b = slip next 2 sts on to cable needle and leave at back of work, k1, then k2 from cable needle;

c3f = slip next st on to cable needle and leave at front of work, k2, then k1 from cable needle;

dec = decrease;

foll = follows;

g st = garter stitch (every row knit);

k = knit; **p** = purl;

patt = pattern;

pw2 = purl next stitch wrapping yarn twice around needle;

rep = repeat;

RS = right side;

sl 1(2)p = slip one(two) stitch(es) purlwise;

st(s) = stitch(es);

tog = together;

WS = wrong side

Note: To join in a new ball of Sari Ribbon, overlap the two ends by 1.5cm (½in) and oversew together securely using matching sewing thread. Cont in patt, knitting the join in when you come to it.

*k4, k into front and back of next st, rep from * to last 3 sts, k3. 80 sts.
Now work patt in reverse as foll:
Next row: (RS) With B, k to end.
Beg with 1st row, cont in patt to match first side before g st panel, ending with 6th row. With B, p 1 row. With A, cast/bind off.

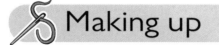 Making up

Make a single twist in the centre of the wrap, through g st panel. Now join cast-on and cast/bound-off edges, with RS of pattern uppermost on both edges.
To finish off raw ends of ribbon yarn, thread through a few stitches on WS. Trim to 1.5cm (½in), fold under raw edge and oversew securely in place using a matching sewing thread.

HOW TO
WORK THE SLIP STITCH AND CABLE PATTERN

The pattern is worked with yarn (A) and ribbon yarn (B).

1 Cast on with yarn A and then work a foundation row of knit stitches with yarn B. Start the first row of the pattern with yarn B. Purl one, then purl the

next stitch wrapping the yarn twice around the needle (abbreviated as pw2 and shown above), purl four. Repeat a sequence of pw2 twice, and purl four to the last two stitches, pw2 and purl one.

2 Pick up yarn A for the second row. Begin with knit one, then slip one purlwise, allowing the extra loop to fall off the left-hand needle (sl 1p), and knit four. Repeat a sequence of slipping two stitches purlwise, allowing the extra loops to fall off the needle (sl 2p), and knit four to the last two stitches. Slip one purlwise, allowing the extra loop to fall off the needle (sl 1p), and knit one.

3 Still with yarn A, begin the third row with purl one, slip one purlwise and purl four. Repeat a sequence of slip two

purlwise and purl four to the last two stitches. Slip one purlwise and purl one.

4 For the fourth row with yarn A, knit one, slip one purlwise and knit four. Repeat a sequence of slip two

purlwise and knit four to the last two stitches, slip one purlwise and knit one.

5 For the fifth row, still with yarn A, repeat the third row.

6 Change to yarn B for the sixth row. Begin with knit one, then slip the next stitch onto a cable needle and leave at the front of the work. Knit the next two stitches and then knit the stitch

on the cable needle (c3f). Slip the next two stitches onto the cable needle and leave at the back of the work. Knit one and then knit the two stitches from the cable needle (c3b). Repeat a sequence of c3f and c3b to the last stitch, knit one.

7 These six rows form the pattern and are repeated as instructed.

Ruffle and lace sweater

With a lean body and ruffles around the neck and bottom, this stunning sweater looks almost like a pierrot costume.

Intricate and sophisticated, this cotton sweater with its narrow vertical lace panels fits neatly over the body and flares out around the hemline and cuffs, ending in elaborate lace ruffles like the neck.

The Yarn

Rowan Handknit Cotton is 100% cotton. It is soft to handle and machine washable. There is a range of interesting colours to choose from including neutrals, pastels and some deep fashion shades.

GETTING STARTED

Fairly easy main fabric but dealing with large number of stitches for ruffle edges can be tricky

Size:

To fit bust: 81–86[91–97:102–107]cm/32–34[36–38:40–42]in

Actual size: 99[111:124]cm/39[43¾:48¾]in

Length: 68[70:72]cm/26¾[27½:28¼]in

Sleeve seam: 46cm (18in)

Note: Figures in square brackets [ ] refer to larger sizes; where there is only one set of figures, it applies to all sizes

How much yarn:

16[19:22] x 50g (2oz) balls of Rowan Handknit Cotton, approx 85m (92 yards) per ball

Needles:

Pair of 4mm (no. 8/US 6) knitting needles

4mm (no. 8/US 6) circular knitting needle, 80cm (32in) long

Additional items:

2.75mm (no. 12/US C) crochet hook

Tension/gauge:

19 sts and 30 rows measure 10cm (4in) square over st st and lace patt on 4mm (no. 8/US 6) needles

IT IS ESSENTIAL TO WORK TO THE STATED TENSION/GAUGE TO ACHIEVE SUCCESS

What you have to do:

Cast on stitches for shoulders and neck edge and work downwards. Work in stocking/stockinette stitch with lacy panels. Work simple shaping for armholes and side edges. Work ruffles at lower edges in rows on circular needle to cope with large number of stitches. Make a picot cast/bound-off edge using crochet hook. Pick up stitches around neckline. Work ruffle collar in rounds on circular needle.

 ## Instructions

Abbreviations:

alt = alternate; **cont** = continue; **dec** = decrease(ing); **foll** = following; **inc** = increase(ing); **k** = knit; **kfb** = knit into front and back of stitch; **patt** = pattern; **p** = purl; **pfb** = purl into front and back of stitch; **psso** = pass slipped stitch over; **rep** = repeat; **RS** = right side; **sl** = slip; **st(s)** = stitch(es); **st st** = stocking/stockinette stitch; **tog** = together; **WS** = wrong side; **yo** = yarn over needle to make a stitch

Note: The sweater is worked from the top down so the ruffle edging grows out of the lines of lace. If necessary, use the circular needle to contain the amount of stitches when working the lower edge ruffles as well as for working the collar ruffle in the round.

BACK:

Cast on 70[80:90] sts.

1st row: (RS) K6[4:2], (yo, p2tog, k5) 8[10:12] times, yo, p2tog, k6[4:2].

2nd row: P6[4:2], (yo, p2tog, p5) 8[10:12] times, yo, p2tog, p6[4:2]. These 2 rows form st st and lace patt. Cont in patt, work 42[46:50] more rows.

** Shape armholes:

Inc row: (RS) Kfb, patt to last 2 sts, kfb, k1. 72[82:92] sts. Taking incs into patt, inc in this way at each end of next 7[8:9] RS rows. 86[98:110] sts. Work 1 row.

Next row: (RS) Patt to end, do not turn, using left thumb loop on 4 sts. 90[102:114] sts.

Next row: Taking cast-on sts into patt, patt to end, do not turn, using left thumb loop on 4 sts. 94[106:118] sts. Cont in patt with 4[3:2] sts in st st at each side, work 28 rows.

Dec row: (RS) K1, k2tog, patt to last 3 sts, sl 1, k1, psso, k1. 92[104:116] sts. Cont in patt, dec in this way on foll 10th row. 90[102:114] sts. Work 13 rows straight.

Inc row: (RS) Kfb, patt to last 2 sts, kfb, k1. 92[104:116] sts. Taking incs into patt, inc in this way at each end of 8[9:10] foll 6th rows. 108[122:136] sts. Work 29[23:17] rows straight.

Ruffle edging:

1st row: (RS) K4, (p2tog, k5) 14[16:18] times, p2tog, k4. 93[105:117] sts.

2nd row: P3, (p2tog, yo, p4) 15[17:19] times. 93[105:117] sts.

3rd row: K4, (yo, k1, yo, k5) 14[16:18] times, yo, k1, yo, k4. 123[139:155] sts.

4th and every WS row: P to end.

5th row: K4, (yo, k3, yo, k5) 14[16:18] times, yo, k3, yo, k4. 153[173:193] sts.

7th row: K4, (yo, k5, yo, k5) 14[16:18] times, yo, k5, yo, k4. 183[207:231] sts.

9th row: K4, (yo, k7, yo, k5) 14[16:18] times, yo, k7, yo, k4. 213[241:269] sts.

11th row: K4, (yo, k9, yo, k5) 14[16:18] times, yo, k9, yo, k4. 243[275:307] sts.

13th row: K to end.

Picot cast/bound-off row: (WS) Insert crochet hook in first stitch, pull loop through and drop st off left needle, * insert hook in next st, pull loop through st and loop on hook, drop st off left needle, make 3 chain, slip stitch in 3rd chain from hook, insert hook in next st, pull loop through st and loop on needle, drop st off left needle, rep from * to end. Fasten off.

FRONT:
Left side:

Cast on 12[17:22] sts.

1st row: (RS) *1st size* K4, yo, p2tog, k6, *2nd size* k4, yo, p2tog, k5, yo, p2tog, k4, *3rd size* k4, (yo, p2tog, k5) twice, yo, p2tog, k2.

2nd row: *1st size* P6, yo, p2tog, p4, *2nd size* p4, yo, p2tog, p5, yo, p2tog, p4, *3rd size* p2, (yo, p2tog, p5) twice, yo, p2tog, p4. These 2 rows form st st and lace patt. Work 8[12:16] more rows.

Shape neck:

1st inc row: (RS) Kfb, patt to end. 13[18:23] sts. Taking incs into patt, inc in this way at beg of next 5 RS rows. 18[23:28] sts.

2nd inc row: (WS) Patt to last 2 sts, pfb, p1. 19[24:29] sts. Inc in this way at neck edge on next 2 rows. 21[26:31] sts. Cut off yarn and leave sts on a holder.

Right side:

Cast on 12[17:22] sts.

1st row: (RS) *1st size* K6, yo, p2tog, k4, *2nd size* k4, yo, p2tog, k5, yo, p2tog, k4, *3rd size* k2, (yo, p2tog, k5) twice, yo, p2tog, k4.

2nd row: *1st size* P4, yo, p2tog, p6, *2nd size* p4, yo, p2tog, p5, yo, p2tog, p4, *3rd size* p4, (yo, p2tog, p5) twice, yo, p2tog, p2. These 2 rows form st st and lace patt. Work 8[12:16] more rows.

Shape neck:

1st inc row: (RS) Patt to last 2 sts, kfb, k1. 13[18:23] sts. Taking incs into patt, inc in this way at end of next 5 RS rows. 18[23:28] sts.

2nd inc row: (WS) Pfb, end. 19[24:29] sts. Inc in this way at neck edge on next 2 rows. 21[26:31] sts.

Joining row: (RS) Patt 21[26:31] sts of right side of neck, using left thumb loop on 28 sts, patt 21[26:31] sts of left side of neck. 70[80:90] sts. Cont in patt, work 19 rows straight. Complete as given for Back from **.

SLEEVES:

Cast on 21[28:35] sts.

1st row: (RS) K6, (yo, p2tog, k5) 2[3:4] times, k1.

2nd row: P6, (yo, p2tog, p5) 2[3:4] times, p1.

These 2 rows set st st and lace patt.

Shape top:

3rd row: (RS) Kfb, patt to end, using left thumb, loop on 2 sts. 24[31:38] sts.

4th row: Pfb, (yo, p2tog, p5) 3[4:5] times, yo, p2tog, using left thumb, loop on 2 sts. 27[34:41] sts.

5th row: Kfb, k1, (yo, p2tog, k5) 3[4:5] times, yo, p2tog, k2, using left thumb, loop on 2 sts. 30[37:44] sts.

6th row: Pfb, p3, (yo, p2tog, p5) 3[4:5] times, yo, p2tog, p3, using left thumb, loop on 2 sts. 33[40:47] sts.

7th row: Kfb, k4, (yo, p2tog, k5) 4[5:6] times, using left thumb, loop on 2 sts. 36[43:50] sts.

8th row: Pfb, p6, (yo, p2tog, p5) 4[5:6] times, p1, using left thumb, loop on 2 sts. 39[46:53] sts.

9th row: Kfb, (yo, p2tog, k5) 5[6:7] times, yo, k3. 41[48:55] sts.
10th row: P2, (yo, p2tog, p5) 5[6:7] times, yo, p2tog, p2.
11th row: Kfb, patt to last 2 sts, kfb, k1. 43[50:57] sts.
Cont in patt, inc in same way as 11th row on next 3 RS rows. 49[56:63] sts. Work 7 rows straight.

Shape armholes:
Inc in same way as 11th row on next row and 7[8:9] foll RS rows. 65[74:83] sts. Work 1 row.
Next row: (RS) Patt to end, do not turn, using left thumb loop on 4 sts. 69[78:87] sts.
Next row: Patt to end, do not turn, using left thumb loop on 4 sts. 73[82:91] sts.
Cont in patt, work 20 rows straight.
Dec row: (RS) K1, k2tog, patt to last 3 sts, sl 1, k1, psso, k1. 71[80:89] sts. Cont in patt, dec in this way on 13[14:15] foll 6th rows. 45[52:59] sts. Work 19[13:7] rows straight.

Ruffle edging:
1st row: (RS) K4, (p2tog, k5) 5[6:7] times, p2tog, k4. 39[45:51] sts.
2nd row: P3, (p2tog, yo, p4) 6[7:8] times. 39[45:51] sts.
3rd row: K4, (yo, k1, yo, k5) 5[6:7] times, yo, k1, yo, k4. 51[59:67] sts.
4th and every WS row: P to end.
5th row: K4, (yo, k3, yo, k5) 5[6:7] times, yo, k3, yo, k4. 63[73:83] sts.
7th row: K4, (yo, k5, yo, k5) 5[6:7] times, yo, k5, yo, k4. 75[87:99] sts.
9th row: K4, (yo, k7, yo, k5) 5[6:7] times, yo, k7, yo, k4. 87[101:115] sts.
11th row: K4, (yo, k9, yo, k5) 5[6:7] times, yo, k9, yo, k4. 99[115:131] sts.
13th row: K to end.
Work picot cast/bound-off as given for Back.

COLLAR:
Matching sts, join shoulder seams.
Using 4mm (no. 8/US 6) circular needle and with WS facing, pick up and k 48 sts across back neck, 18[25:32] sts down right front neck, 28 sts across front neck and 18[25:32] sts up left front neck. 112[126:140] sts.
1st round: (RS) K2, (p2, k5) to last 5 sts, p2, k3.
2nd round: K2, (yo, p2tog, k5) to last 5 sts, yo, p2tog, k3.
3rd round: K2, (k2tog, yo, k5) to last 5 sts, k2tog, yo, k3.
4th round: As 2nd round.
5th round: As 3rd round.
6th round: K2, (p2tog, k5) to last 5 sts, p2tog, k3. 96[108:120] sts.
7th round: K2, (yo, k2tog, k4) to last 4 sts, yo, k2tog, k2.

8th round: K2, (yo, k1, yo, k5) to last 4 sts, yo, k1, yo, k3. 128[144:160] sts.
9th and every alt round: K to end.
10th round: K2, (yo, k3, yo, k5) to last 6 sts, (yo, k3) twice. 160[180:200] sts.
12th round: K2, (yo, k5) to last 3 sts, yo, k3. 192[216:240] sts.
14th round: K2, (yo, k7, yo, k5) to last 10 sts, yo, k7, yo, k3. 224[252:280] sts.
16th round: K2, (yo, k9, yo, k5) to last 12 sts, yo, k9, yo, k3. 256[288:320] sts.
18th round: K2, (yo, k11, yo, k5) to last 14 sts, yo, k11, yo, k3. 288[324:360] sts.
20th round: K2, (yo, k13, yo, k5) to last 16 sts, yo, k13, yo, k3. 320[360:400] sts.
K 2 rounds. Turn, work picot cast/bind-off as given for Back.

Making up

Press according to directions on ball band. Set in sleeves. Join side and sleeve seams.

Long tubular scarf

Practise knitting in the round and make this striped scarf.

This simple scarf is a long length of tubular stocking/stockinette stitch fabric with a clever use of two colours in stripes of varying widths that reverse at mid-point.

GETTING STARTED

 This is a good exercise for working in rounds

Size:
Scarf is approximately 13cm wide x 114cm long (5in x 45in)

How much yarn:
2 x 50g (2oz) balls of Debbie Bliss Baby Cashmerino, approx 125m (137 yards) per ball, in colour A
2 balls in colour B

Needles:
Set of four 3.25mm (no. 10/US 3) double-pointed knitting needles

Tension/gauge:
25 sts and 34 rows measure 10cm (4in) square over st st on 3.25mm (no. 10/US 3) needles
IT IS ESSENTIAL TO WORK TO THE STATED TENSION/ GAUGE TO ACHIEVE SUCCESS

What you have to do:
Cast on all stitches and divide between three needles, using fourth needle of set to work with. Work throughout in rounds of stocking/stockinette stitch to produce a tubular fabric. Follow directions to work two-colour stripes in varying widths.

The Yarn
Debbie Bliss Baby Cashmerino is a soft blend of 55% merino wool, 33% microfibre and 12% cashmere. It can be machine washed at a low temperature and there is a wide choice of fabulous colours for stripes.

Abbreviations:
cm = centimetre(s);
cont = continue;
foll = follows; **k** = knit;
rep = repeat;
st(s) = stitch(es);
st st = stocking/
stockinette stitch

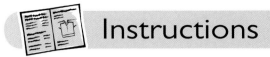

Instructions

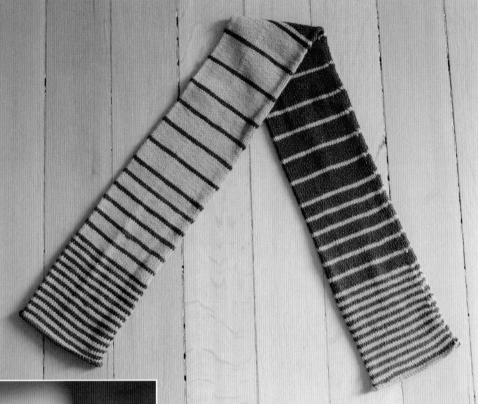

SCARF:

With A, cast on 66 sts. Divide sts evenly between three needles and join into a round. Using fourth needle to work with, k 1 round. Cont throughout in rounds of st st (every round k), working striped sections as foll:

Narrow-stripe section:

(48 rounds)

Work 2 rounds B and 2 rounds A. Rep these 4 rounds 11 times more.

Medium-stripe section:

(48 rounds)

Work 6 rounds B and 2 rounds A. Rep these 8 rounds 5 times more.

Wide-stripe section:

(48 rounds)

Work 10 rounds B and 2 rounds A. Rep these 12 rounds 3 times more.

Very wide stripe section:

(96 rounds)

Work 14 rounds B and 2 rounds A. Rep these 16 rounds twice more.

Work 2 rounds in B and 14 rounds in A. Rep these 16 rounds twice more.

Wide-stripe section:

(48 rounds)

Work 2 rounds B and 10 rounds A. Rep these 12 rounds 3 times more.

Medium-stripe section:

(48 rounds)

Work 2 rounds B and 6 rounds A. Rep these 8 rounds 5 times more.

Narrow-stripe section:

(48 rounds)

Work 2 rounds B and 2 rounds A. Rep these 4 rows 11 times more. Work 2 more rounds in B, then cast/bind off.

Press tubular scarf flat, according to directions on ball band.

Striped chair cushion

Paint an old wooden chair and add this zingy cushion/ pillow to create a favourite relaxing spot.

Update a traditional chair with this brightly-striped cushion/pillow. Worked in wide stripes of stocking/ stockinette stitch, it has gusseted sides to take a foam seat pad and knitted ties to hold it in place.

The Yarn

Debbie Bliss Cotton Double Knitting is 100% pure cotton. It is a high-quality yarn, that can be machine washed, and is ideal for the wear and tear of a seat cushion/ pillow. There are a number of bright shades in the range for your own striking colour combinations.

 Instructions

Abbreviations:

beg = beginning; **cm** = centimetre(s); **cont** = continue; **k** = knit; **rep** = repeat; **RS** = right side; **st(s)** = stitch(es); **st st** = stocking/stockinette stitch; **WS** = wrong side

TOP AND BOTTOM PANELS: (Make 2)

With 4mm (no. 8/US 6) needles and B, cast on 62 sts.
Beg with a k row, work 8 rows in st st.
Cont in st st, work in stripe sequence of 8 rows each A and B.
Rep last 16 rows 5 times more, ending with a WS row.
Cast/bind off.

GETTING STARTED

 Simple, basic striped fabric but making up cover requires attention for a neat finish

Size:

Cushion/pillow is 43cm long x 35cm wide x 6cm deep (17in x 13¾in x 2½in)

How much yarn:

4 x 50g (2oz) balls of Debbie Bliss Cotton Double Knitting, approx 84m (92 yards) per ball, in main colour A 3 balls in contrast colour B

Needles:

Pair of 4mm (no. 8/US 6) knitting needles Two short 4mm (no. 8/US 6) double-pointed needles

Additional items:

Foam pad to fit cover

Tension/gauge:

17 sts and 24 rows measure 10cm (4in) square over st st on 4mm (no. 8/US 6) needles IT IS ESSENTIAL TO WORK TO THE STATED TENSION/ GAUGE TO ACHIEVE SUCCESS

What you have to do:

Work in stocking/stockinette stitch and simple horizontal stripe sequence. Carry colour not in use loosely up side of work. Make tubular ties on double-pointed needles.

GUSSET:
With 4mm (no. 8/US 6) needles and A, cast on 12 sts. Beg with a k row, cont in st st until strip, when slightly stretched, fits all around outer edges of panels, ending with a WS row. Cast/bind off.

TIES: (Make 2)
With 4mm (no. 8/US 6) double-pointed needles and B, cast on 4 sts. K 1 row, then push sts to other end of needle, pull yarn tightly across back of sts and k to end. Cont in this way, to form tubular cord, until tie measures 30cm (12in). Cast/bind off.

Making up

Block pieces to shape and press according to directions on ball band. Join cast-on and cast/bound-off edges of gusset. With seam at centre of back edge and RS facing, pin gusset around one panel and sew in place, using A. Repeat with the other panel, leaving the back edge open. Insert the foam pad and neatly slipstitch the seam closed. Fold the ties in half and attach the folded edges – one to each upper back corner.

HOW TO
MAKE AN I-CORD

Knit two 30cm (12in) tubular cords to attach the cushion/pillow to the back of the chair.

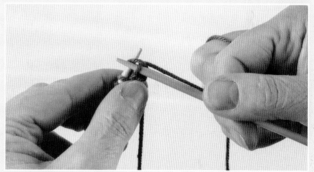

2 Knit one row so the stitches are all on the right-hand needle and then push the stitches to the other end of the needle and place it in your left hand, without turning the needle.

3 Begin the next row. The yarn will be at the opposite end of the row so pull it across the back of the stitches to start the new row.

4 Continue in this way, sliding the stitches to the other end of the needle as you complete each row and taking the yarn across the back of the stitches to form a tube of knitting. When the tube measures 30cm (12in), cast/bind off knitwise.

I To make one cord, use a pair of double-pointed needles. Cast on four stitches in the usual way, using the thumb method.

Cardigan with lace bands

With bands of lace and a picot edging, this cardigan is unashamedly pretty.

This cardigan with three-quarter sleeves has bands of openwork lace pattern on a stocking/stockinette stitch background and picot edgings.

The Yarn
Sublime Soya Cotton DK is a blend of 50% soya and 50% cotton. It is a unique natural yarn with a luxurious drape that is very soft next to the skin. There is an unusual palette of some spicy, rich shades and contrasting cool, watery colours.

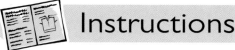

Instructions

Abbreviations:
alt = alternate; **beg** = beginning; **cm** = centimetre(s); **cont** = continue; **dec** = decrease; **foll** = follow(s)(ing); **inc** = increase; **k** = knit; **p** = purl; **psso** = pass slipped stitch over; **rem** = remain(ing); **rep** = repeat; **RS** = right side; **sl** = slip; **st(s)** = stitch(es); **st st** = stocking/stockinette stitch; **tog** = together; **WS** = wrong side; **yfwd** = yarn forward/yarn over to make a stitch

BACK:
With 3.25mm (no. 10/US 3) needles cast on 99[107:115] sts loosely.
1st row: (RS) K2, (p1, k1) to last st, k1.
2nd row: K1, (p1, k1) to end.
Rep these 2 rows twice more.

GETTING STARTED

Straightforward style although openwork pattern may take some practise

Size:
To fit bust: 86[91:97]cm/34[36:38]in
Actual size: 90[97:104.5]cm/35½[38:41]in
Length: 57[58:60]cm/22½[23:23½]in
Sleeve seam: 26.5cm (10½in)
Note: Figures in square brackets [ ] refer to larger sizes; where there is only one set of figures, it applies to all sizes

How much yarn:
9[9:10] x 50g (2oz) balls of Sublime Soya Cotton DK, approx 110m (120 yards) per ball

Needles:
Pair of 3.25mm (no. 10/US 3) knitting needles
Pair of 4mm (no. 8/US 6) knitting needles

Additional items:
Stitch holder
8 buttons

Tension/gauge:
22 sts and 28 rows measure 10cm (4in) square over st st on 4mm (no. 8/US 6) needles
IT IS ESSENTIAL TO WORK TO THE STATED TENSION/GAUGE TO ACHIEVE SUCCESS

What you have to do:
Work hems in single (knit one, purl one) rib. Work main fabric in stocking/stockinette stitch with bands of openwork mesh. Use simple shaping for armholes, neck and sleeve tops. Finish edges of ribbed bands with decorative picot cast/bind-off.

Change to 4mm (no. 8/US 6) needles. Beg with a k row, work 15 rows in st st. ** Work mesh lace band as foll:

1st row: (WS) P1, (k1, p3) to last 2 sts, k1, p1.

2nd row: K2, (yfwd, sl 1, k2tog, psso, yfwd, k1) to last st, k1.

3rd row: As 1st row.

4th row: K3, (yfwd, sl 1, k1, psso, k2) to end.

5th–15th rows: Rep 1st–4th rows twice, then 1st–3rd rows again.

Beg with a k row, work 21 rows in st st. **

Rep from ** to ** once more, then work 1st–15th rows of mesh lace band again.***

K 1 row and p 1 row.

Shape armholes:

Cont in st st only, cast/bind off 6[7:8] sts loosely at beg of next 2 rows. Dec 1 st at each end of next 3[3:5] rows, then at each end of every foll alt row until 75[79:85] sts rem. Work straight until armholes measure 18[19:21] cm/7[7½:8¼]in from beg, ending with a p row.

Shape shoulders:

Cast/bind off 6[7:7] sts loosely at beg of next 4 rows and 7[6:8] sts at beg of next 2 rows. Cut off yarn.

Leave rem 37[39:41] sts on a holder.

RIGHT FRONT:

With 3.25mm (no. 10/US 3) needles cast on 47[51:55] sts. Work as given for Back to ***. K 1 row, p 1 row and k 1 row.

**** Shape armhole:

Cont in st st only, cast/bind off 6[7:8] sts loosely at beg of next row. Dec 1 st at armhole edge on next 3[3:5] rows, then on every foll alt row until 35[37:40] sts rem. Work straight until Front measures 11[13:14]cm/4½[5:5½]in from beg of armhole, ending at front edge.

Shape neck:

Cast/bind off 11[12:13] sts loosely at beg of next row. Dec 1 st at neck edge on next 5 rows. 19[20:22] sts. Work straight until Front measures same as Back to shoulder, ending at armhole edge.

Shape shoulder:

Cast/bind off 6[7:7] sts at beg of next and foll alt row. Work 1 row. Cast/bind off rem 7[6:8] sts.

LEFT FRONT:

With 3.25mm (no. 10/US 3) needles cast on 47[51:55] sts. Work as given for Back to ***. K 1 row and p 1 row. Now complete as given for Right front from **** to end.

SLEEVES: (Make 2)

With 3.25mm (no. 10/US 3) needles cast on 51[55:63] sts loosely. Work 6 rows in k1, p1 rib as given for Back. Change to 4mm (no. 8/US 6) needles. Beg with a k row, work 15 rows in st st, inc 1 st at each end of 7th and 13th[1st, 5th, 9th and 13th:1st, 5th, 9th and 13th] rows.

55[63:71] sts.

Now work 1st–15th rows of mesh lace band as given for Back, inc 1 st at each end of 4th and 10th rows. 59[67:75] sts.

Beg with a k row, work 21 rows in st st, inc 1 st at each end of 1st, 7th, 13th and 19th rows. 67[75:83] sts.

Now work 1st–15th rows of mesh lace band again, inc 1 st at each end of 4th and 10th rows. 71[79:87] sts.

K 1 row and p 1 row.

Shape top:

Cont in st st only, cast/bind off 6[7:8] sts loosely at beg of next 2 rows. Dec 1 st at each end of next and every foll alt row until 29[33:35] sts rem, then at each end of every row until 19[23:25] sts rem. Cast/bind off loosely.

NECKBAND:

Join shoulder seams.

With 3.25mm (no. 10/US 3) needles and RS of work facing, pick up and k 29[30:33] sts evenly up right front neck, k across back neck sts on holder and pick up and k 29[30:33] sts evenly down left front neck. 95[99:107] sts.

Beg with a 2nd row, work 6 rows in rib as given for Back. Cast/bind off to form picot edge as foll: *Cast/bind off 2 sts, sl st on right needle back on to left needle, cast on 2 sts, cast/bind off 2 sts, k2tog, sl 2nd st on right over first st, rep from * to last 2 sts, cast/bind off 2 sts, fasten off.

BUTTON BAND:

With 3.25mm (no. 10/US 3) needles cast on 9 sts. Cont in rib as given for Back until strip, when slightly stretched, fits up Left front to top of neckband. Cast/bind off in rib.

Sew band in place. Mark positions of 8 buttons, the first and last to be in 3rd/4th rows from upper and lower edges, and others evenly spaced between.

BUTTONHOLE BAND:

Work as given for Button band, making buttonholes to correspond with markers as foll:

1st buttonhole row: (RS) Rib 3, cast/bind off 3 sts in rib, rib to end.

2nd buttonhole row: Rib to end, casting on 3 sts over those cast/bound off in previous row. Sew band in place.

PICOT BORDERS:

With 3.25mm (no. 10/US 3) needles and RS of Back facing, k up one st from every rib st at cast-on edge. Work picot cast/bind-off row as given for Neckband. Work similar picot border on lower Front and Sleeve edges.

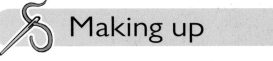

Making up

Do not press. Sew in sleeves. Join side and sleeve seams. Sew on buttons.

Lacy evening scarf

Add the finishing touch to your evening outfit with this delicate silk scarf.

Knitted in a beautiful silk yarn, this long scarf is worked in a simple lace pattern that forms undulating scalloped ridges. The ends are accentuated with long fringes and sewn-on beads.

GETTING STARTED

 The lace design is very simple as only one row out of four is patterned

Size:
Scarf is approximately 12cm wide x 150cm long (4¾in x 59in), excluding fringes

How much yarn:
2 x 50g (2oz) hanks of Debbie Bliss Pure Silk, approx 125m (136 yards) per hank

Needles:
Pair of 5mm (no. 6/US 8) knitting needles

Additional items:
Crochet hook for fringing
Approximately 70 small pearl beads (optional)
Approximately 100 small purple beads (optional)
Sewing needle and matching thread

Tension/gauge:
30 sts and 18 rows measure 10cm (4in) square over lace patt, stretched slightly lengthways, on 5mm (no. 6/ US 8) needles
IT IS ESSENTIAL TO WORK TO THE STATED TENSION/ GAUGE TO ACHIEVE SUCCESS

What you have to do:
Work in lace pattern using decorative increasing and decreasing. Add fringe to each end. Sew on beads (optional).

The Yarn
Debbie Bliss Pure Silk is 100% silk. It is a luxurious yarn in a double knitting (light worsted) weight that has the subtle pearlised sheen of silk and it can be hand washed. There are plenty of gorgeous colours to choose from.

Abbreviations:
beg = beginning;
cm = centimetre(s);
cont = continue;
foll = follows; **k** = knit;
p = purl; **patt** = pattern;
RS = right side;
st(s) = stitch(es);
tog = together;
yfwd = yarn forward/yarn
over between stitches to
make a stitch

Instructions

SCARF:

Cast on 36 sts loosely. Cont in lace patt as foll:
1st row: (RS) K to end.
2nd row: P to end.
3rd row: *(K2tog) 3 times, (yfwd, k1) 6 times, (k2tog) 3 times, rep from * once more.
4th row: K to end. These 4 rows form patt. Cont in patt until work measures about 150cm (59in) from beg, ending with a 4th patt row. Cast/bind off loosely.

Making up

Press according to directions on ball band, gently stretching knitting lengthways to accentuate the scallops of lace patt.
Fringe:
Cut 38 lengths of yarn, each 26cm (10in) long. With crochet hook and using one strand of yarn each time, knot fringes along cast-on and cast/bound-off edges, working into each corner st and then into alternate sts.
Beading:
At one end of scarf, highlight the first four garter-stitch ridges in the pattern by sewing on about 35 pearl beads and 50 purple beads at random. Repeat at the other end of the scarf.

HOW TO
WORK THE LACY PATTERN

This is a very simple lace pattern with decorative increases and decreases worked on one row of the four-row pattern.

1 Cast on thirty-six stitches loosely. The cast-on row is worked in this way because the pattern creates a scalloped effect. If the cast-on row is too tight, then this constrains the scalloped effect. Knit the first row and then purl the second row.

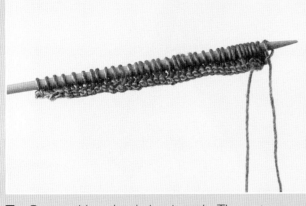

2 For the third row, knit two stitches together three times, bring the yarn forward/yarn over between the needles and knit one. Repeat this five times more and then knit two stitches together three times. Repeat this complete sequence once more.

3 Knit the fourth row to the end; this completes the four-row pattern.

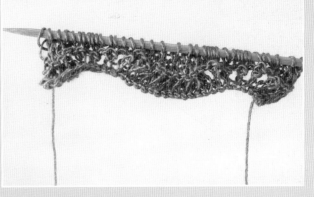

4 The four-row pattern forms a scalloped lace effect. Here you can see the pattern emerging after eight rows. Continue repeating these four rows until the scarf measures 150cm (59in) ending with a fourth row. Cast/bind off loosely in order to maintain the scalloped effect.

Classic waistcoat

This waistcoat/vest has a wonderful retro feel – play up the vintage look by choosing a colour like this mustard yellow.

Worked in stocking/stockinette stitch in an Aran (fisherman) wool yarn, this traditional piece with curved front edges will be a winner in your wardrobe.

GETTING STARTED

 Worked in basic fabric but shaping requires concentration

Size:
To fit bust: 81–86[91–97:102–107]cm/32–34[36–38:40–42]in
Actual size: 86[97:108]cm/34[38:42½]in
Length at centre back: 54[57:59]cm/21¼[22½:23¼]in
Note: Figures in square brackets [ ] refer to larger sizes; where there is only one set of figures, it applies to all sizes

How much yarn:
7[7:8] x 50g (2oz) balls of Debbie Bliss Rialto Aran, approx 80m (87 yards) per ball

Needles:
Pair of 4.5mm (no. 7/US 7) knitting needles
Pair of 5mm (no. 6/US 8) knitting needles

Additional items:
5 buttons, Stitch holders and markers

Tension/gauge:
18 sts and 24 rows measure 10cm (4in) square over st st on 5mm (no. 6/US 8) needles
IT IS ESSENTIAL TO WORK TO THE STATED TENSION/ GAUGE TO ACHIEVE SUCCESS

What you have to do:
Work main fabric in stocking/stockinette stitch. Shape curved lower edges of fronts with groups of cast-on stitches. Work pocket linings and inset pockets. Use fashioned shapings for armholes and neck. Pick up stitches and work edgings in single rib, making eyelet buttonholes.

The Yarn
Debbie Bliss Rialto Aran contains 100% merino wool. It has a slight twist that gives good stitch definition for stocking/stockinette-stitch fabrics and it can be machine washed at a low temperature. There are about 20 fabulous shades to choose from.

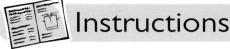 Instructions

Abbreviations:
alt = alternate; **beg** = beginning; **cm** = centimetre(s); **cont** = continue; **dec** = decrease(ing); **foll** = following; **k** = knit; **p** = purl; **psso** = pass slipped stitch over; **rem** = remain; **rep** = repeat; **RS** = right side; **sl** = slip; **st(s)** = stitch(es); **st st** = stocking/stockinette stitch; **tbl** = through back of loops; **tog** = together; **WS** = wrong side; **yrn** = yarn round/yarn over needle to make a stitch

BACK:

With 5mm (no. 6/US 8) needles cast on 79[89:99] sts. Beg with a k row, work 76[80:82] rows in st st, ending with a p row.

Shape armholes:

Cast/bind off 3[4:5] sts at beg of next 2 rows.

Next row: K2, k2tog, k to last 4 sts, sl 1, k1, psso, k2.

Next row: P to end.

Rep last 2 rows 5[7:9] times more. 61[65:69] sts. Work 36[34:32] rows straight, ending with a p row.

Shape shoulders:

Cast/bind off 17[18:19] sts at beg of next 2 rows. 27[29:31] sts.

Change to 4.5mm (no. 7/US 7) needles.

Next row: K1, (p1, k1) to end.

Next row: P1, (k1, p1) to end.

Rep last 2 rows twice more. Cast/bind off in rib.

POCKET LININGS: (Make 2)

With 5mm (no. 6/US 8) needles cast on 15[15:17] sts. Beg with a k row, work 19[21:21] rows in st st, ending with a k row. Cut off yarn and leave sts on a holder.

LEFT FRONT:

With 5mm (no. 6/US 8) needles cast on 16[17:18] sts. P 1 row. Beg with a k row, cont in st st, casting on 2 sts at beg of next 8[10:12] rows. 32[37:42] sts.*

Keeping side edge straight, cast on 1 st at beg (front edge) of foll 5 alt rows. 37[42:47] sts. Place a marker at front edge of last row. Beg with a k row, work 4 rows straight.

Work pocket top:

Next row: (RS) K11[14:15], p1, (k1, p1) 7[7:8] times, k11[13:15].

Next row: P11[13:15], k1, (p1, k1) 7[7:8] times, p11[14:15].

Rep last 2 rows once more.

Next row: K11[14:15], cast/bind off next 15[15:17] sts firmly in rib, k to end.

Next row: P11[13:15], with WS facing p across 15[15:17] sts from pocket lining, p to end.

Work 50[54:56] rows straight, ending with a p row. Place a marker at front edge of last row.

Shape neck and armhole:

Next row: K to last 4 sts, sl 1, k1, psso, k2.

Work 3 rows straight.

Next row: Cast/bind off 3[4:5] sts, k to last 4 sts, sl 1, k1, psso, k2.

Next row: P to end.

Next row: K2, k2tog, k to end.

Next row: P to end.

Next row: K2, k2tog, k to last 4 sts, sl 1, k1, psso, k2.

Rep last 4 rows 2[3:4] times more. 23[24:25] sts. Keeping armhole edge straight, cont to dec at neck edge as before on foll 4th rows until 17[18:19] sts rem. Work 13[11:9] rows straight, ending at armhole edge. Cast/bind off.

RIGHT FRONT:

Work as given for Left front to *. Keeping side edge straight, cast on 1 st at beg (front edge) of next and foll 4 alt rows. 37[42:47] sts. Place a marker at front edge of last row. Beg with a p row, work 5 rows straight.

Work pocket top:

Next row: (RS) K11[13:15], p1, (k1, p1) 7[7:8] times, k11[14:15].

Next row: P11[14:15], k1, (p1, k1) 7[7:8] times, p11[13:15].

Rep last 2 rows once more.

Next row: K11[13:15], cast/bind off next 15[15:17] sts firmly in rib, k to end.

Next row: P11[14:15], with WS facing p across 15[15:17] sts from pocket lining, p to end.

Work 50[54:56] rows straight, ending with a p row. Place a marker at front edge of last row.

Shape neck and armhole:

Next row: K2, k2tog, k to end.

Work 3 rows straight.

Next row: K2, k2tog, k to end.

Next row: Cast/bind off 3[4:5] sts, p to end.

Next row: K to last 4 sts, sl 1, k1, psso, k2.

Next row: P to end.

Next row: K2, k2tog, k to last 4 sts, sl 1, k1, psso, k2.

Next row: P to end.

Rep last 4 rows 2[3:4] times more. 23[24:25] sts. Keeping armhole edge straight, cont to dec at neck edge as before on 3rd and foll 4th rows until 17[18:19] sts rem. Work 14[12:10] rows straight, ending at armhole edge. Cast/bind off.

EDGINGS:

Lower back:

With 4.5mm (no. 7/US 7) needles and RS of work facing, pick up and k79[89:99] sts along lower edge of back. Beg with a WS row, work 5 rows in k1, p1 rib as given for back neckband. Cast/bind off in rib.

Armholes:

Join shoulder seams. With 4.5mm (no. 7/US 7) needles and RS of work facing, pick up and k81[87:93] sts evenly around armhole edge. Work 5 rows in k1, p1 rib as before. Cast/bind off in rib.

Right front:

With 4.5mm (no. 7/US 7) needles and RS of work facing, pick up and k10[12:14] sts from side edge to cast-on edge, 1 st in corner, 16[17:18] sts along cast-on edge, 1 st in corner, 19[21:23] sts round curve to first marker, 1 st in corner, 48[50:52] sts up to second marker, 1 st in corner and 41[42:43] sts up neck to shoulder. 138[146:154] sts.

Next 2 rows: (K1, p1) to end.

Buttonhole row: (WS) (K1, p1) 21[22:23] times, (yrn, p2tog tbl, rib 10) 4 times, yrn, p2tog tbl, rib to end. Rib 2 more rows. Cast/bind off in rib.

Left front:

Work to match right front, omitting buttonholes.

 Making up

Press according to directions on ball band. Join side and all edging seams. Sew pocket linings in place on WS of work. Sew on buttons.

Heart-shaped cushion

This is a challenging knit, but the reward is a truly individual item for your home!

With its inset motif in a mohair yarn and textured embellishments of bobbles and a cord trim, this heart-shaped cushion/pillow is a work of art that is worth the effort.

The Yarn

Sirdar Denim Tweed DK (background) contains 60% acrylic, 25% cotton and 15% wool. The two-tone shades give the yarn a slightly variegated appearance. Sirdar Juniper (bobbles and cord) contains 53% acrylic, 27% wool and 20% polyester. It is fashion yarn full of different colours and textures. Sirdar Blur (inset heart) is a mixture of 70% acrylic and 30% kid mohair and has a soft, brushed appearance.

GETTING STARTED

Shaping and intarsia make this a challenge for a competent knitter

Size:
Cushion/pillow is 47.5cm deep x 41cm across widest point (18½in x 16in)

How much yarn:
3 x 50g (2oz) balls of Sirdar Denim Tweed DK, approx 170m (186 yards) per ball, in main colour A
1 x 50g (2oz) ball of Sirdar Juniper, approx 60m (66 yards) per ball, in contrast colour B
1 x 50g (2oz) ball of Sirdar Blur, approx 190m (207 yards) per ball, in contrast colour C

Needles:
Pair of 4mm (no. 8/US 6) knitting needles
Pair of 5mm (no. 6/US 8) double-pointed knitting needles

Additional items:
4 buttons, 41cm (16in) heart cushion pad/pillow form

Tension/gauge:
22 sts and 28 rows measure 10cm (4in) square over st st on 4mm (no. 8/US 6) needles
IT IS ESSENTIAL TO WORK TO THE STATED TENSION/GAUGE TO ACHIEVE SUCCESS

What you have to do:
Work front in stocking/stockinette stitch, shaping to form heart. Incorporate bobbles in a different yarn into rows at intervals. Work intarsia heart motif in a different textured yarn. Make an i-cord in same yarn as bobbles and sew to front in a heart shape. Make backs in two pieces with ribbed button and buttonhole bands.

 Instructions

Abbreviations:

alt = alternate; **beg** = beginning; **cm** = centimetre(s); **cont** = continue; **dec** = decrease(ing); **foll** = follow(s)(ing); **inc** = increase(ing); **k** = knit; **p** = purl; **psso** = pass slipped stitch over; **rem** = remain; **rep** = repeat; **RS** = right side; **sl** = slip; **st(s)** = stitch(es); **st st** = stocking/stockinette stitch; **tbl** = through back of loops; **tog** = together; **WS** = wrong side; **yfwd** = yarn forward/yarn over to make a stitch

FRONT:

With 4mm (no. 8/US 6) needles and A, cast on 2 sts. Beg with a k row, cont in st st and work 4 rows, inc 1 st at each end of 2nd, 3rd and 4th rows. 8 sts. K 1 row. Inc 1 st at each end of next 2 rows. Work 1 row. Rep last 3 rows 7 times more. 40 sts. Inc 1 st at each end of next and foll alt row. 44 sts.

Place bobbles:

Next row: (RS) K22, make bobble (MB) as foll: join in B, into next st work k1, (p1, k1) twice so making 5 sts, turn and beg with a p row, work 4 rows in st st on these 5 sts, turn and p2tog, p1, p2tog, turn and with A, k3tog, k21. Inc 1 st at each end of next and every foll alt row until there are 56 sts.

Place intarsia heart motif:
Next row: (RS) K18 A, MB, 8 A, 2 C, 8 A, MB, 18 A.
Next row: Inc in 1st st, p26 A, 2 C, 26 A, inc in last st. 58 sts.
Next row: K27 A, 4 C, 27 A.
Next row: Inc in 1st st, p26 A, 4 C, 26 A, inc in last st. 60 sts.
Next row: K27 A, 6 C, 27 A.
Next row: Inc in 1st st, p26 A, 6 C, 26 A, inc in last st. 62 sts.
Cont in this way, working 2 more sts in C on next and foll RS rows and inc 1 st at each end of WS rows until there are 68 sts.
Next row: K18 A, MB, 8 A, 14 C, 8 A, MB, k18 A.
Next row: Inc in 1st st, p26 A, p14 C, p26 A, inc in last st. 70 sts.
Next row: K27 A, k16 C, k27 A.
Next row: P27 A, p16 C, p27 A.
Next row: Inc in 1st st, k25 A, 18 C, 25 A, inc in last st. 72 sts.
Next row: P27 A, 18 C, 27 A.
Next row: K26 A, 20 C, 26 A.
Next row: Inc in 1st st, p25 A, 20 C, 25 A, inc in last st. 74 sts.
Next row: K26 A, 22 C, 26 A.
Next row: P26 A, 22 C, 26 A.
Next row: Inc in 1st st, k24 A, 24 C, 24 A, inc in last st. 76 sts.
Next row: P26 A, 24 C, 26 A.
Next row: K17 A, MB, 7 A, 26 C, 7 A, MB, 17 A.
Next row: Inc in 1st st, p24 A, 26 C, 24 A, inc in last st. 78 sts.
Next row: K25 A, 28 C, 25 A.
Next row: P25 A, 28 C, 25 A.
Next row: Inc in 1st st, k23 A, 30 C, 23 A, inc in last st. 80 sts.
Next row: P25 A, 30 C, 25 A.
Next row: K24 A, 32 C, 24 A.
Next row: Inc in 1st st, p23 A, 32 C, 23 A, inc in last st. 82 sts.
Next row: K24 A, 34 C, 24 A.
Next row: P24 A, 34 C, 24 A.
Next row: Inc in 1st st, k22 A, 36 C, 22 A, inc in last st. 84 sts.
Next row: P24 A, 36 C, 24 A.
Next row: K15 A, MB, 8 A, 36 C, 8 A, MB, k15 A.
Next row: Inc in 1st st, p23 A, 36 C, 23 A, inc in

last st. 86 sts.
Next row: K25 A, 36 C, 25 A.
Next row: P25 A, 36 C, 25 A.
Next row: Inc in 1st st, k24 A, 17 C, 2 A, 17 C, 24 A, inc in last st. 88 sts.
Next row: P26 A, 17 C, 2 A, 17 C, 26 A.
Next row: K26 A, 17 C, 2 A, 17 C, 26 A.
Next row: P26 A, 16 C, 4 A, 16 C, 26 A.
Next row: K27 A, 15 C, 4 A, 15 C, 27 A.
Next row: Inc in 1st st, p26 A, 15 C, 4 A, 15 C, 26 A, inc in last st. 90 sts.
Next row: K29 A, 13 C, 6 A, 13 C, 29 A.
Next row: P30 A, 11 C, 8 A, 11 C, 30 A.
Next row: K31 A, 9 C, 10 A, 9 C, 31 A.
Next row: P33 A, 5 C, 14 A, 5 C, 33 A.
Next row: Inc in 1st st, k11 A, MB, 64 A, MB, 11 A, inc in last st. 92 sts. With A, p 1 row.
Next row: K46 A, MB, 45 A.
Beg with a p row, work 9 rows straight in A.
Next row: K16 A, MB, 17 A, MB, 22 A, MB, 17 A, MB, 16 A. With A, p 1 row.
Next row: Sl 1, k1, psso, k to last 2 sts, k2tog. 90 sts.
Beg with a p row, work 3 rows in st st in A.
Next row: Sl 1, k1, psso, k21 A, MB, 42 A, MB, 21 A, k2tog. 88 sts. Cont in A only and beg with a p row, work 5 rows in st st, dec 1 st at each end of 3rd row. 86 sts.

Divide and shape top:
**Next row: Sl 1, k1, psso, k40, turn and cont on these 41 sts for 1st side. P1 rpw.
 Next row: Sl 1, k1, psso, k to end. 40 sts

Next row: P2tog, p to end. 39 sts.
Next row: Sl 1, k1, psso, k to end. 38 sts
* Beg with a p row, work 7 rows, dec 1 st at each end of every row. 24 sts. Cast/bind off 3 sts at beg of next 2 rows and 4 sts at beg of foll 2 rows. Cast/bind off rem 10 sts. With RS facing, rejoin yarn to rem sts and cast/bind off next 2 sts, k to last 2 sts, k2tog. 41sts. P 1 row.
Next row: K to last 2 sts, k2tog. 40 sts
Next row: P to last 2 sts, p2tog. 39 sts
Next row: K to last 2 sts, k2tog. 38 sts
Complete as 1st side from * to end.

CORD:

With 5mm (no. 6/US 8) double-pointed needles and B, cast on 5 sts. K 1 row.
Next row: * Without turning work and RS facing, slide sts to other end of needle and, pulling yarn from left-hand side of sts to right across back, k1 tbl, k4. * Rep from * to *, remembering to pull yarn tightly across back and always working a k row, until cord measures approximately 112cm (44in) when slightly stretched. Cast/bind off.

BACK:
Lower section:

With 4mm (no. 8/US 6) needles and A, cast on 2 sts. Beg with a k row, cont in st st and work 5 rows, inc 1 st at each end of 2nd, 3rd and 4th rows. 8 sts. Now inc 1 st at each end of next 2 rows. Work 1 row straight. Rep last 3 rows 7 times more. 40 sts. Inc 1 st at each end of next and every foll alt row until there are 70 sts, then at each end of every foll 3rd row until there are 82 sts. Work 2 rows straight.

Button band:

Next row: (RS) Inc in 1st st, k1, (p2, k2) to last 4 sts, p2, k1, inc in last st. 84 sts
Next row: P3, (k2, p2) to last 5 sts, k2, p3.
Next row: K3, (p2, k2) to last 5 sts, p2, k3.
Next row: Inc in 1st st, p2, patt to last 5 sts, k2, p2, inc in last st. 86 sts
Next row: K4, patt to last 6 sts, p2, k4.
Next row: P4, patt to last 6 sts, k2, p4.
Next row: Inc in 1st st, k3, patt to last 6 sts, p2, k3, inc in last st. 88 sts
Next row: P5, patt to last 7 sts, k2, p5.
Next row: K5, patt to last 7 sts, p2, k5.
Next row: P5, patt to last 7 sts, k2, p5. Cast/bind off in patt.

Top section:

With 4mm (no. 8/US 6) needles and A, cast on 84 sts.

Buttonhole band:

Next row: K3, (p2, k2) to last 5 sts, p2, k3.
Next row: P3, (k2, p2) to last 5 sts, k2, p3.
Next row: K3, patt to last 5 sts, p2, k3.
Next row: Inc in 1st st, p2, patt to last 5 sts, k2, p2, inc in last st. 86 sts
Next row: K4, rib 8, yfwd, p2tog, (rib 18, yfwd, p2tog) 3 times, rib 8, k4.
Next row: P4, patt to last 6 sts, k2, p4.
Next row: Inc in 1st st, k3, patt to last 6 sts, p2, k3, inc in last st. 88 sts
Next row: P5, patt to last 7 sts, k2, p5.
Next row: K5, patt to last 7 sts, p2, k5.
Next row: P5, patt to last 7 sts, k2, p5.
Beg with a k row, cont in st st and work 7 rows, inc 1 st at each end of 2nd and 7th rows. 92 sts. Work 13 rows straight.
Next row: Sl 1, k1, psso, k to last 2 sts, k2tog. 90 sts.
Beg with a p row, work 9 rows in st st, dec 1 st at each end of 4th and 7th rows. 86 sts.

Divide and shape top:

Work as given for Front from ** to end.

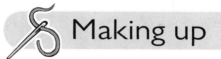

Making up

Stretching cord slightly, sew it to cushion/pillow front halfway between bobbles and edge, following heart shape. Place front WS down and lay backs on top with RS facing and overlapping button bands. Sew around the outer edge, then turn RS out. Sew on buttons. Insert cushion pad/pillow form and button to close.

Flower hatband

Turn a store-bought hat into a designer look with this amazing knitted flower and hatband.

All you need to decorate a plain hat with a creative floral arrangement is some simple knitting and sewing skills.

GETTING STARTED

Easy shapes and stitches; take care with assembly for a neat finished result

Size:

Band: 60cm (24in) long (adjustable); *Flower motif (with leaves):* approximately 17cm wide x 18cm deep (6¾in x 7in)

How much yarn:

1 x 100g (3½oz) ball of Patons 100% Cotton DK, approx 210m (230 yards) per ball, in colour A

1 x 100g (3½oz) ball of Patons 100% Cotton 4-ply, approx 330m (360 yards) per ball, in colour B

1 x 50g (2oz) ball of Sirdar Just Bamboo, approx 94m (103 yards) per ball, in colour C

Needles:

Pair of 3mm (no. 11/US 2) knitting needles
Pair of 4mm (no. 8/US 6) knitting needles

Additional items:

0.6mm (24 gauge) silver-plated beading wire
Pack of 6mm (¼in) black glass beads
25cm (10in) of wired organza ribbon 38mm (1½in) wide
Black button 27mm (1⅛in) in diameter
Sewing needle and thread

Tension/gauge:

23 sts and 34 rows measure 10cm (4in) square over st st using DK cotton on 3mm (no. 11/US 2) needles

What you have to do:

Work hatband in moss/seed stitch. Work patterned flower centre using two ends of yarn. Make separate petals in stocking/stockinette stitch using simple shaping. Work leaves in stocking/stockinette stitch. Wire leaves and make decorative beaded wires, then assemble and stitch flower motif on hatband.

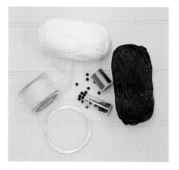

The Yarn

Patons 100% Cotton in 4-ply (fingering) and DK (light worsted weight) is pure cotton. It is available in plenty of colours. Sirdar Just Bamboo is 100% bamboo. It is a flat tape yarn in muted pastel shades that will add texture to the floral motif.

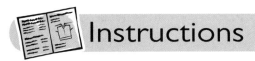 Instructions

Abbreviations:

beg = beginning;

cm = centimetre(s);

cont = continue;

dec = decrease(ing);

inc = increase(ing);

k = knit; **p** = purl;

psso = pass slipped stitch over; **rem** = remain(ing);

rep = repeat;

RS = right side;

sl = slip; **st(s)** = stitch(es);

st st = stocking/stockinette stitch;

tbl = through back of loops;

tog = together;

yo = yarn over needle to make a stitch

HATBAND:

With 3mm (no. 11/US 2) needles and A, cast on 10 sts.

1st row: (K1, p1) to end.

2nd row: (P1, k1) to end. Rep these 2 rows to form moss/seed st until band measures 60cm (24in), or fits around hat, when slightly stretched. Either graft sts together or cast/bind off and join ends of band with mattress st.

FLOWER MOTIF:

Central flower:

With 4mm (no. 8/US 6) needles and one end of B and C tog, cast on 57 sts.

1st row: P to end.

2nd row: K2, *k1, sl this st back on to left needle and pass next 8 sts on left needle over it and off needle, (yo) twice, k first st again, k2, rep from * to end.

3rd row: P1, *p2tog, p into front of first yo and into back of second yo, p1, rep from * to last st, p1. 22 sts.

4th row: K to end.

5th row: *P2tog, rep from * to end. 11 sts.

6th row: *K2, pass second st over first, rep from * to last st, k1. Cut off yarn. Thread through rem 6 sts, pull up tightly and sew edges of flower tog.

Petals: (Make 12)

With 3mm (no. 11/US 2) needles and A, cast on 6 sts. P 1 row.

Next row: K1, inc in next st, k2, inc in next st, k1. 8 sts. Beg with a p row, work 3 rows in st st.

Next row: K1, inc in next st, k4, inc in next st, k1. 10 sts. Beg with a p row, work 9 rows in st st.

Next row: (K2tog tbl) twice, k2, (k2tog) twice. 6 sts.

Next row: P2tog, p2, p2tog. 4 sts. Cast/bind off. Sew in yarn end at finish, but leave yarn at base of petal for sewing on to band later.

Leaves: (Make 4)

With 3mm (no. 11/US 2) needles and two ends of B tog, cast on 3 sts. Beg with a k row, cont in st st, inc 1 st at each end of every RS row until there are 9 sts. Work 11 rows straight, ending with a p row.

Dec row: Sl 1, k1, psso, k to last 2 sts, k2tog. Cont to dec in this way on every foll RS row until 3 sts rem. Work 1 row.

Next row: Sl 1, k1, psso, k1 and cast/bind off one st. Fasten off.

so that leaves extend beyond petals, and sew in place. Finish off by folding organza ribbon into a loop and adding to arrangement as shown.

Making up

Press all petals and leaves to correct shape. Wire leaves by threading wire through sts at back, bending back in a loop at point. Note that two leaves will need extra-long wires extending from base so that they extend beyond petals.

For lower beaded wires, take a 30cm (12in) length of wire and thread bead to centre, fold wire in half, bending wire so that bead stays in place. Repeat with two other – 20cm (8in) and 14cm (5½in) – lengths of wire, then wrap another length of wire around all three at base to hold group in place. For upper beaded wires, make two beaded wires – using 20cm (8in) and 14cm (5½in) lengths – and bind tog as described above.

Working over seam and using photograph as a guide, position two leaves and beaded wires on hatband. Pin and sew in place. Pin and sew first layer of six petals in place, then make another layer of remaining petals, alternating position of petals with first layer. Sew flower to centre of arrangement and sew on button to centre of flower. Pin and place two lower leaves with wire at back of hatband,

Beaded mohair bag

Tiny beads, a beaded fringe and a flower-shaped clasp are the motifs of this pretty cross-body bag.

Worked in a glamorous yarn and patterned with beads, this pretty bag with its decorative knitted clasp, beaded fringes and long cord strap is ideal for evening occasions.

GETTING STARTED

No difficult shaping, but knitting with beads may take some practise

Size:

Bag is approximately 15cm wide x 17.5cm high (6in x 7in), excluding fringing

How much yarn:

1 x 50g (2oz) ball of Patons Orient, approx 150m (164 yards) per ball

Needles:

Pair of 4mm (no. 8/US 6) knitting needles
Pair of 4mm (no. 8/US 6) double-pointed needles

Additional items:

Approximately 508 beads with large enough hole to thread on to yarn
Sewing needle and thread
20cm x 46cm (8in x 18in) piece of lining fabric
Press stud (popper snap)

Tension/gauge:

22 sts and 30 rows measure 10cm (4in) square over st st on 4mm (no. 8/US 6) needles
IT IS ESSENTIAL TO WORK TO THE STATED TENSION/ GAUGE TO ACHIEVE SUCCESS

What you have to do:

Thread beads on to yarn. Work bag in stocking/ stockinette stitch with beaded panel as instructed. Make flower motif for 'clasp'. Knit cord strap for handle and sew on beaded fringes along lower edge. Sew lining for bag as instructed.

The Yarn

Patons Orient contains 50% polyamide, 30% acrylic and 15% mohair. Its slight brushed appearance is enhanced with a glinting metallic thread that gives the finished fabric a beautiful sheen. There is a small range of classic deep and pale colours to choose from.

Abbreviations:

beg = beginning;
cm = centimetre(s);
cont = continue;
foll = follow(s)(ing);
k = knit; **p** = purl;
psso = pass slipped
stitch over;
rem = remain(ing);
rep = repeat;
RS = right side; **sl** = slip;
st(s) = stitch(es);
st st = stocking/
stockinette stitch;
tbl = through back
of loop;
tog = together;

Note: Before starting work, thread 217 beads on to yarn. Take a length of sewing thread, fold it in half and thread the two cut ends into a sewing needle. Insert end of knitting yarn through loop of sewing thread, then thread beads on to needle and slide down over sewing thread and doubled end of knitting yarn. Push beads a long way along yarn so that you have plenty of yarn for knitting first section before starting to place beads.

Instructions

BAG:
With 4mm (no. 8/US 6) needles cast on 35 sts. K 2 rows.
Beg with a k row, cont in st st until work measures 11cm (4½in) from beg, ending with a WS row. Cont in bead patt as foll:
1st row: (RS) K2, (bring yarn to front of work, slide bead up yarn to needle, sl next st purlwise, take yarn to back holding bead in front of slipped st – called place bead (pb), k1) to last 3 sts, pb, k2.
2nd row: P to end.
3rd row: K3, (pb, k1) to last 4 sts, pb, k3.
4th row: P to end.
Rep these 4 rows 3 times more. Beg with a k row, cont in st st until work measures 35cm (13¾in) from beg, ending with a WS row.
Shape flap:
1st row: K1, sl 1, k1, psso, (pb, k1) to last 4 sts, pb, k2tog, k1.
2nd row: P1, p2tog, p to last 3 sts, p2tog, p1.

3rd row: K1, sl 1, k1, psso, k1, (pb, k1) to last 3 sts, k2tog, k1.
4th row: P to end.
5th row: As 3rd row.
6th row: As 2nd row.
7th row: K1, sl 1, k1, psso, (pb, k1) to last 4 sts, pb, k2tog, k1.
8th row: P to end.
Rep last 2 rows 7 times more. 9 sts.
23rd row: K1, sl 1, k1, psso, pb, k1, pb, k2tog, k1.
24th row: P to end.
25th row: K1, sl 1, k1, psso, pb, k2tog, k1. 5 sts. P 1 row. Cast/bind off.

FLOWER:
Before starting work, thread 5 beads on to yarn as before.
With 4mm (no. 8/US 6) needles cast on 8 sts.
1st row: (RS) Sl 1, k7.
2nd row: Sl 1, k5 (2 sts rem on left-hand needle), turn and take yarn to back.

3rd row: Sl 1, k3 (2 sts rem on left-hand needle), turn and take yarn to back.

4th row: Sl 1, k3, turn.

5th row: Sl 1, k1, pb, k3 (0 sts rem on left-hand needle), turn.

6th row: Sl 1, k6 (1 st on left-hand needle), turn.

7th row: Sl 1, then start by using this st, cast/bind off all sts until 1 st rem, turn.

8th row: Cast on 7 sts.

Rep these 8 rows 3 times more, then work 1st–7th rows again to make 5 petals in all. Fasten off, leaving a long length of yarn.

Sew first petal to last petal to create a flower. Sew running sts through sts at inner edge of central hole and draw up to close the hole. Fasten off.

CORD STRAP:

With 4mm (no. 8/US 6) double-pointed needles cast on 3 sts. K 1 row.

Next row: * Without turning work and RS facing, slide sts to other end of needle and, pulling yarn from left-hand side of sts to right across back, k1 tbl, k2. *
Rep from * to *, remembering to pull yarn tightly across back and always working a k row, until cord measures 140cm (55in) or length required to fit across body. Cast/bind off.

 Making up

Using bag as a template, cut out lining fabric, adding 1.5cm (⅝in) seam allowance on all sides.

With WS facing, fold up cast-on edge of bag by 17cm (6½in) and join side seams. Sew ends of cord strap securely to side seams inside top edge of bag. Turn bag RS out. Sew 5 beads to centre and 5 to edges of each flower petal, then sew flower to point of flap.

Fringing:

Make 32 beaded fringes as foll: Take a 20cm (8in) length of yarn and knot close to one end. Thread on 2 beads and knot again, then thread on another 6 beads. Thread yarn into a tapestry needle and sew fringe through lower edge of bag, securing and knotting on inside of bag to leave approximately 5cm (2in) hanging. Place a fringe to the side of every stitch along lower edge of bag.

Lining:

Fold 1.5cm (⅝in) to WS along short, straight edge of lining and sew in place. With RS facing and taking 1.5cm (⅝in) seam allowances, fold lining as for knitted bag, join side seams and trim seams close to stitching. Place lining inside bag, with WS tog, and sew through lower corners with sewing thread to secure in place. Slip stitch folded edge of lining along inside top edge of bag. Fold under remaining free edges of lining along flap and slip stitch in place.

Sew a press stud (popper snap) to underside of flower and flap point and corresponding section to front of bag.

Long skinny cardigan

A classic design is given a twist with extra-large buttons and a small rever collar.

This long-line cardigan in stocking/stockinette stitch has a deep V-neckline and a small rever collar. It fastens with three large buttons just below the neckline.

GETTING STARTED

Basic stocking/stockinette stitch fabric but shaping needs concentration

Size:
To fit bust: 81–86[91–97:102–107]cm/32–34[36–38:40–42]in
Actual size at bust: 90[101:112]cm/35½[37¾:44]in
Length: 78[82.5:87]cm/30¾[32½:34¼]in
Sleeve seam: 42.5[44.5:46.5]cm/16¾[17½:18¼]in
Note: Figures in square brackets [ ] refer to larger sizes; where there is only one set of figures, it applies to all sizes

How much yarn:
11[12:13] x 50g (2oz) balls of Sublime Angora Merino DK, approx 119m (130 yards) per ball

Needles:
Pair of 3.75mm (no. 9/US 5) knitting needles
Pair of 4mm (no. 8/US 6) knitting needles

Additional items:
Stitch holders and markers, 3 large buttons

Tension/gauge:
22 sts and 28 rows measure 10cm (4in) square over st st on 4mm (no. 8/US 6) needles
IT IS ESSENTIAL TO WORK TO THE STATED TENSION/GAUGE TO ACHIEVE SUCCESS

What you have to do:
Work welts, cuffs, front bands and collar in single (k1, p1) rib. Work main fabric in stocking/stockinette stitch. Use simple shaping for darts, armhole and front edge. Work inset pockets. Shape rever collar with turning rows.

The Yarn
Sublime Angora Merino DK contains 80% extra fine merino wool and 20% angora. This combination of fibres feels soft and luxurious and there are eleven fabulous colours to choose from.

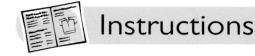

Instructions

Abbreviations:
alt = alternate; **beg** = beginning; **cm** = centimetre(s); **cont** = continue; **dec** = decrease(ing); **foll** = follow(s)(ing); **inc** = increase(ing); **k** = knit; **m1** = make one stitch by picking up strand lying between needles and working into back of it; **p** = purl; **psso** = pass slipped stitch over; **rem** = remain(ing); **rep** = repeat; **RS** = right side; **sl** = slip; **st(s)** = stitch(es); **st st** = stocking/stockinette stitch; **tbl** = through back of loop(s); **tog** = together; **WS** = wrong side

BACK:
With 3.75mm (no. 9/US 5) needles cast on 105[117:129] sts.
1st row: (RS) K1, (p1, k1) to end.
2nd row: P1, (k1, p1) to end. Rep these 2 rows twice more. Change to 4mm (no. 8/US 6) needles. Beg with a k row, cont in st st and work 62[68:74] rows.

Shape hips:
Dec row: (RS) K8, sl 1, k1, psso, k to last 10 sts, k2tog, k8. Work 5 rows in st st. Rep last 6 rows 6 times more, then work dec row again. 89[101:113] sts. Work 9[11:13] rows straight, ending with a p row.

Shape bust:
Inc row: (RS) K4, m1, k to last 4 sts, m1, k4.
Work 5 rows in st st. Rep last 6 rows 4 times more, then work inc row again. 101[113:125] sts. Work 9[11:13] rows straight, ending with a p row.

Shape armholes:
Cast/bind off 4[5:6] sts at beg of next 2 rows. 93[103:113] sts.
Next row: K1, sl 1, k1, psso, k to last 3 sts, k2tog, k1.
Next row: P to end. Rep last 2 rows 5[6:7] times more, then work 1st of them again. 79[87:95] sts. Work 45 rows straight, ending with a p row.

Shape shoulders:
Cast/bind off 7[8:9] sts at beg of next 6 rows.
Cast/bind off rem 37[39:41] sts.

POCKET LININGS: (Make 2)
With 4mm (no. 8/US 6) needles cast on
25[27:29] sts. Beg with a k row, work 31[33:35]
rows in st st, ending with a k row. Cut off yarn
and leave sts on a holder.

LEFT FRONT:
With 3.75mm (no. 9/US 5) needles cast on
49[55:61] sts. Work 6 rows in k1, p1 rib as
given for Back.
Change to 4mm (no. 8/US 6) needles. Beg with
a k row, cont in st st and work 52[56:60] rows.
Work pocket top:
Next row: (RS) K12[14:16], p1, (k1, p1)
12[13:14] times, k12[14:16].
Next row: P12[14:16], k1, (p1, k1) 12[13:14] times,
p12[14:16]. Rep last 2 rows once more.
Next row: K12[14:16], cast/bind off next 25[27:29] sts
firmly in rib, k to end.
Next row: P12[14:16], with WS facing, p across 25[27:29]
sts of pocket lining, p to end.
Work 4[6:8] rows in st st, ending with a p row.*
Shape hips:
Dec row: (RS) K8, sl 1, k1, psso, k to end.
Work 5 rows in st st. Rep last 6 rows 6 times more, then
work dec row again. 41[47:53] sts. Work 9[11:13] rows
straight, ending with a p row.
Shape bust:
Inc row: (RS) K4, m1, k to end. Work 5 rows straight. Rep
last 6 rows twice more 44[50:56] sts.
Shape neck:
1st row: (RS) K4, m1, k to last 3 sts, k2tog, k1.
2nd row: P to end.
3rd row: K to end.
4th row: P1, p2tog, p to end.
5th row: K to end.
6th row: P to end.
Rep last 6 rows twice more. 41[47:53] sts. Cont to dec
1 st at neck edge as set on next and every foll 6th row,
AT SAME TIME work 4[6:8] rows keeping side edge
straight, ending at armhole edge.
Shape armhole:
Cast/bind off 4[5:6] sts at beg of next row. P 1 row.
Next row: (RS) K1, sl 1, k1, psso, work to end.

**Keeping neck shapings correct, dec 1 st at armhole
edge on foll 6[7:8] alt rows. 26[30:33] sts. Keeping armhole
edge straight, cont to dec at neck edge until 21[24:27] sts
rem. Work 15[13:11] rows straight, ending with a p row.
Shape shoulder:
Cast/bind off 7[8:9] sts at beg of next and foll alt row.
Work 1 row. Cast/bind off rem 7[8:9] sts.

RIGHT FRONT:
Work as Left front to *.
Shape hips:
Dec row: (RS) K to last 10 sts, k2tog, k8.
Work 5 rows in st st. Rep last 6 rows 6 times more, then
work dec row again. 41[47:53] sts. Work 9[11:13] rows
straight, ending with a p row.
Shape bust:
Inc row: (RS) K to last 4 sts, m1, k4. Work 5 rows straight.
Rep last 6 rows twice more 44[50:56] sts.
Shape neck:
1st row: (RS) K1, sl 1, k1, psso, k to last 4 sts, m1, k4.
2nd row: P to end.
3rd row: K to end.
4th row: P to last 3 sts, p2tog tbl, p1.
5th row: K to end.
6th row: P to end.
Rep last 6 rows twice more. 41[47:53] sts. Cont to dec
1 st at neck edge as set on next and every foll 6th row,
AT SAME TIME work 5[7:9] rows keeping side edge
straight, ending at armhole edge.

Shape armhole:
Cast/bind off 4[5:6] sts at beg of next row.

Next row: (RS) Work to last 3 sts, k2tog, k1.
Work as Left front from ** to end, working 1 row more before shoulder shaping.

SLEEVES: (Make 2)
With 3.75mm (no. 9/US 5) needles cast on 53[57:61] sts.
Work 8 rows in k1, p1 rib as given for Back.
Change to 4mm (no. 8/US 6) needles.
Inc row: (RS) K4, m1, k to last 4 sts, m1, k4.
Beg with a p row, work 9[9:7] rows in st st, ending with a p row. Rep last 10[10:8] rows 8[10:12] times more, then work inc row again. 73[81:89] sts. Work 21[7:19] rows straight, ending with a p row.

Shape top:
Cast/bind off 4[5:6] sts at beg of next 2 rows. Dec 1 st at each end of next and 3 foll 4th rows, then on every foll alt row until 37[41:45] sts rem, ending with a p row. Dec 1 st at each end of every row until 21 sts rem. Cast/bind off.

FRONT BANDS AND COLLAR:
Knitted all in one piece, beg at lower edge of Left front band. Join shoulder seams.
With 3.75mm (no. 9/US 5) needles cast on 13 sts.
1st row: (RS) K2, (p1, k1) to last st, k1.
2nd row: K1, (p1, k1) to end.
Rep last 2 rows until band, when slightly stretched, fits up to beg of front neck shaping, ending with a WS row. Place 1st marker at end of last row.

Shape for collar:
Keeping rib correct, inc 1 st at beg of next row (shaped edge) and every foll alt row to 33 sts, ending with a RS row.
Next row: (WS) Rib 20, turn, sl 1, rib to end.
Work 4 rows across all sts, inc as before at beg of 2nd and 4th rows. 35 sts.
Next row: (WS) Rib 22, turn, sl 1, rib to end.
Work 4 rows across all sts, inc as before at beg of 2nd and 4th rows. 37 sts.
Next row: (WS) Rib 24, turn, sl 1, rib to end.
Work 4 rows across all sts, inc as before at beg of 2nd and 4th rows. 39 sts.
Next row: (WS) Rib 26, turn, sl 1, rib to end.
Work 4 rows across all sts, inc as before at beg of 2nd and 4th rows. 41 sts.
Next row: (WS) Rib 28, turn, sl 1, rib to end.

Work 4 rows across all sts, inc as before at beg of 2nd and 4th rows. 43 sts.
Place 2nd marker at shaped edge of last row.
* Next row: (WS) Rib 30, turn, sl 1, rib to end.
Work 4 rows straight across all sts. Cont as set from * until shaped edge of collar fits up to left shoulder. Place 3rd marker at shaped edge of last row. Cont as set until shaped edge of collar fits across back neck to right shoulder. Place 4th marker at shaped edge of last row. Now cont straight as set for same number of rows as worked between 2nd and 3rd markers, ending after turning rows. Work 4 rows across all sts, dec 1 st at beg of 2nd and 4th rows. 41 sts.
Next row: (WS) Rib 28, turn, sl 1, rib to end.
Work 4 rows across all sts, dec 1 st at beg of 2nd and 4th rows. 39 sts.
Next row: (WS) Rib 26, turn, sl 1, rib to end.
Work 4 rows across all sts, dec 1 st at beg of 2nd and 4th rows. 37 sts.
Next row: (WS) Rib 24, turn, sl 1, rib to end.
Work 4 rows across all sts, dec 1 st at beg of 2nd and 4th rows. 35 sts.
Next row: (WS) Rib 22, turn, sl 1, rib to end.
Work 4 rows across all sts, dec 1 st at beg of 2nd and 4th rows. 33 sts.
Next row: (WS) Rib 20, turn, sl 1, rib to end.
Cont in rib across all sts, dec 1 st as set on every foll alt row until 13 sts rem.
Place 5th marker at shaped edge of last row.
Mark position on Left front band of 3 buttons, first one 10 rows below 1st marker (to allow for roll of collar) and rem two at approximately 16-row intervals, or as desired. Cont straight in rib on these 13 sts, working buttonholes at marked positions as foll:
1st buttonhole row: Rib 5, cast/bind off next 3 sts, rib to end.
2nd buttonhole row: Rib to end, casting on 3 sts over those cast/bound off in previous row.
Cont in rib until band fits down to lower edge of Right front. Cast/bind off in rib.

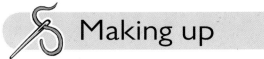

Making up

Sew on front bands and collar, matching 1st and 5th markers to beg of neck shapings and 3rd and 4th markers to left and right shoulders. Catch down pocket linings to WS of fronts. Sew in sleeves. Join side and sleeve seams. Sew on buttons.

Party pashmina

Add a glamorous touch to any outfit with this silky
pashmina knitted in a lacy pattern.

There's no need to spend a fortune on a pashmina for that special occasion when you can make this dramatic wrap in a luxurious silky yarn and stunning lace pattern. Generous fringes at either end add a dramatic touch.

GETTING STARTED

Simple strip of knitting but concentration needed to keep lace pattern correct

Size:
Pashmina is 48cm wide x 184cm long (19in x 72½in), excluding fringing

How much yarn:
10 x 50g (2oz) balls of Sirdar Flirt DK, approx 95m (104 yards) per ball

Needles:
Pair of 3.25mm (no. 10/US 3) knitting needles
Pair of 4mm (no. 8/US 6) knitting needles

Additional items:
Crochet hook

Tension/gauge:
22 sts and 28 rows measure 10cm (4in) square over st st on 4mm (no. 8/US 6) needles
IT IS ESSENTIAL TO WORK TO THE STATED TENSION/ GAUGE TO ACHIEVE SUCCESS

What you have to do:
Work a few rows in garter stitch (every row knit) at each end for borders. Work throughout in lacy pattern featuring decorative increasing and decreasing. Knot a fringe along short ends.

The Yarn
Sirdar Flirt DK is a mixture of 80% bamboo with 20% wool. It has a tight twist and lustrous sheer that give it it distinctive silky appearance. There is a range of glamorous shades including five trendy metallics.

Abbreviations:

cm = centimetre(s);
cont = continue;
foll = follows;
k = knit; **p** = purl;
patt = pattern;
psso = pass slipped
stitch over;
rep = repeat;
sl = slip; **st(s)** = stitch(es);
st st = stocking/
stockinette stitch;
tog = together;
WS = wrong side;
yfwd = yarn forward/yarn
over between needles to
make a stitch

Instructions

PASHMINA:

With 3.25mm (no. 10/US 3) needles cast on 107 sts.
K5 rows.
Change to 4mm (no. 8/US 6) needles. Cont in patt as foll:
1st row: (WS) K3, p to last 3 sts, k3.
2nd row: K4, *yfwd, k3, sl 1, k2tog, psso, k3, yfwd, k1, rep from * to last 3 sts, k3.
3rd row: K3, p to last 3 sts, k3.
4th row: K3, p1, *k1, yfwd, k2, sl 1, k2tog, psso, k2, yfwd, k1, p1, rep from * to last 3 sts, k3.
5th row: K4, *p9, k1, rep from * to last 3 sts, k3.
6th row: K3, p1, *k2, yfwd, k1, sl 1, k2tog, psso, k1, yfwd, k2, p1, rep from * to last 3 sts, k3.
7th row: As 5th row.
8th row: K3, p1, *k3, yfwd, sl 1, k2tog, psso, yfwd, k3, p1, rep from * to last 3 sts, k3.
These 8 rows form patt. Cont in patt until work measures 183cm (72in), ending with an 8th patt row.
Change to 3.25mm (no. 10/US 3) needles. K4 rows.
Cast/bind off knitwise.

Making up

If necessary, press lightly on WS using a warm iron over a dry cloth.

Fringe:

Wrap yarn loosely around a strip of cardboard 28cm (11in) wide. Cut strands along one edge and remove from card. Taking six strands together each time, fold in half, then use a crochet hook to pull strands from front to back through first st in one short end. Pass ends through folded loop and pull to tighten knot. Rep along both short ends, spacing fringes evenly about 4–5 sts apart.

HOW TO
WORK THE LACY PATTERN

Here is a sample of the lace pattern, working the second pattern repeat across a reduced width.

1 Cast on the required number of stitches, knit five rows and work one pattern repeat. For the first pattern row, knit three, purl to the last three stitches and then knit three.

2 Begin the second row with knit four. Work the following sequence; yarn forward/ yarn over, knit three, slip one, knit two together, pass slip stitch over, knit three, yarn forward/yarn over and knit one. Repeat this sequence to the last three stitches and then knit these.

3 The third row is a repeat of the first row. For the fourth row, begin with knit three and then purl one. Work the following sequence; knit one, yarn forward/ yarn over, knit two, slip one, knit two together, pass slip stitch over, knit two, yarn forward/ yarn over, knit one and purl one. Repeat sequence to the last three stitches and then knit these.

4 For row five, begin with knit four. Then purl nine and knit one and repeat this to the last three stitches. Knit three.

5 Begin the sixth row with knit three and purl one. Work the following sequence; knit two, yarn forward/yarn over, knit one, slip one, knit two together, pass slip stitch over, knit one, yarn forward/ yarn over, knit two and purl one. Repeat this sequence to the last three stitches and then knit three.

6 The seventh row is a repeat of the fifth row. For the eighth row, begin with knit three and purl one. Work the following sequence; knit three, yarn forward/ yarn over, slip one, knit two together, pass slip stitch over, yarn forward/yarn over, knit three and purl one. Repeat this sequence to the last three stitches and then knit three.

7 Repeat these eight rows to form the pattern and you will see the solid diamonds and openwork diamond shapes emerging.

Long gloves with ribbed cuffs

Keep out the chill and look cool at the same time with these classic long gloves.

With their long ribbed cuffs featuring a buttoned opening, these stocking/stockinette stitch gloves in a soft 4-ply yarn are an essential fashion accessory.

The Yarn

Tess Dawson Merino 4-ply (fingering) contains 100% merino wool. This easy-care, superwash yarn is luxuriously soft and is available in a palette of six delicious colours.

GETTING STARTED

Easy fabric but pay attention when shaping thumb and fingers

Size:
To fit an average woman's hand

How much yarn:
2 x 50g (2oz) balls of Tess Dawson Merino 4-ply, approx 200m (218 yards) per ball

Needles:
Pair of 3mm (no. 11/US 2) knitting needles
Pair of 3.25mm (no. 10/US 3) knitting needles

Additional items:
2 buttons

Tension/gauge:
28 sts and 36 rows measure 10cm (4in) square over st st on 3.25mm (no. 10/US 3) needles
IT IS ESSENTIAL TO WORK TO THE STATED TENSION/GAUGE TO ACHIEVE SUCCESS

What you have to do:
Work long cuff in double (k2, p2) rib, decreasing for better fit. Work main part of gloves in stocking/stockinette stitch, increasing within fabric for thumb gusset. Shape thumb, then continue on main part of hand before shaping each finger individually. Leave opening at lower edge of cuff, fastening with a button and sewn button loop.

 Instructions

Abbreviations:
beg = beginning; **cm** = centimetre(s); **cont** = continue; **dec** = decrease(ing); **foll** = following; **k** = knit; **m1** = make one stitch by picking up strand lying between needles and knitting into back of it; **p** = purl; **rem** = remaining; **rep** = repeat; **RS** = right side; **st(s)** = stitch(es); **st st** = stocking/stockinette stitch; **tog** = together; **WS** = wrong side

RIGHT GLOVE:
**With 3.25mm (no. 10/US 3) needles cast on 60 sts.
1st row: (RS) K3, *p2, k2, rep from * to last st, k1.
2nd row: K1, p2, *k2, p2, rep from * to last st, k1.
These 2 rows form rib. Cont in rib for a further 12 rows, ending with a WS row and placing a marker at each end of

last row. Keeping rib correct, dec 1 st at each end of next and 4 foll 10th rows. 50 sts. Work 9 more rows, ending with a WS row.

Change to 3mm (no. 11/US 2) needles. Work a further 19 rows in rib, ending with a RS row. Change to 3.25mm (no. 10/US 3) needles.

Next row: (WS) P7, p2tog, (p15, p2tog) twice, p7. 47 sts. Beg with a k row, work in st st for 4 rows, ending with a WS row.**

Shape thumb gusset:

Next row: (RS) K24, m1, k3, m1, k20. 49 sts. Work 3 rows.

Next row: K24, m1, k5, m1, k20. 51 sts. Work 3 rows.

Next row: K24, m1, k7, m1, k20. 53 sts. Work 3 rows.

Next row: K24, m1, k9, m1, k20. 55 sts. Work 3 rows.

Next row: K24, m1, k11, m1, k20. 57 sts. Work 3 rows.

Next row: K24, m1, k13, m1, k20. 59 sts. Work 3 rows, ending with a WS row.

Shape thumb:

Next row: (RS) K39, turn and cast on 2 sts.

Next row: P17, turn and cast on 2 sts.

***Cont on these 19 sts and work 16 rows, ending with a WS row.

Next row: K2, k2tog, (k4, k2tog) twice, k3. 16 sts.

Next row: Purl.

Next row: (K2tog) 8 times.

Cut off yarn, thread through rem 8 sts, pull up tightly and fasten off securely. Join thumb seam.

With RS facing, rejoin yarn and pick up and k 5 sts from base of thumb, k to end. 49 sts. Cont on these 49 sts and work 13 rows, ending with a WS row.

Shape first finger:

Next row: (RS) K32, turn and cast on 1 st.

Next row: P16, turn and cast on 1 st.

Cont on these 17 sts and work 22 rows, ending with a WS row.

Next row: K2, (k2tog, k3) 3 times. 14 sts.

Next row: Purl.

Next row: (K2tog) 7 times.

Cut off yarn, thread through rem 7 sts, pull up tightly and fasten off securely. Join finger seam.

Shape second finger:

With RS facing, rejoin yarn and pick up and k 3 sts from base of first finger, k6, turn and cast on 1 st.

Next row: P16, turn and cast on 1 st. Cont on these 17 sts and work 24 rows, ending with a WS row.

Next row: K2, (k2tog, k3) 3 times. 14 sts.

Next row: Purl.

Next row: (K2tog) 7 times.

Cut off yarn, thread through rem 7 sts, pull up tightly and fasten off securely.

Join finger seam.

Shape third finger:

With RS facing, rejoin yarn and pick up and k 3 sts from base of second finger, k6, turn and cast on 1 st.

Next row: P16, turn and cast on 1 st.

Cont on these 17 sts and work 22 rows, ending with a WS row.

Next row: K2, (k2tog, k3) 3 times. 14 sts.

Next row: Purl.

Next row: (K2tog) 7 times.

Cut off yarn, thread through rem 7 sts, pull up tightly and fasten off securely.

Join finger seam.

Shape fourth finger:

With RS facing, rejoin yarn and pick up and k 5 sts from base of third finger, k5.

Next row: P15. Cont on these 15 sts and work 18 rows, ending with a WS row.

Next row: K1, (k2tog, k3) twice, k2tog, k2. 12 sts.

Next row: Purl.

Next row: (K2tog) 6 times.

Cut off yarn, thread through rem 6 sts, pull up tightly and fasten off securely.***

LEFT GLOVE:

Work as given for Right glove from ** to **.

Shape thumb gusset:

Next row: (RS) K20, m1, k3, m1, k24. 49 sts.

Work 3 rows.

Next row: K20, m1, k5, m1, k24. 51 sts.

Work 3 rows.

Next row: K20, m1, k7, m1, k24. 53 sts.

Work 3 rows.

Next row: K20, m1, k9, m1, k24. 55 sts.

Work 3 rows.

Next row: K20, m1, k11, m1, k24. 57 sts.

Work 3 rows.

Next row: K20, m1, k13, m1, k24. 59 sts.

Work 3 rows, ending with a WS row.

Shape thumb:

Next row: (RS) K35, turn and cast on 2 sts.

Next row: P17, turn and cast on 2 sts.

Complete as given for Right glove from *** to ***.

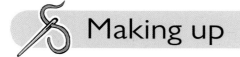 Making up

Do not press.

Join fourth finger seams and side seams to markers, leaving rows above markers open. Make a button loop at top edge of one side of each glove, then sew on buttons to other side to correspond with loops.

Hot-water bottle cover

Go traditional with this cosy cover that will keep you warm on chilly nights.

Two colours worked in bands of traditional Fair Isle patterns look very attractive on this hot-water bottle cover, which is shaped in rib around the top and ties up with a drawstring cord.

GETTING STARTED

 Main fabric is good practise for working Fair Isle patterns

Size:
Cover is 28cm (11in) from neck to base x 45cm (17¾in) all around

How much yarn:
2 x 50g (2oz) balls of British Breeds Blueface Leicester DK, approx 100m (100 yards) per ball, in main colour A
1 ball in contrast colour B

Needles:
Pair of 4mm (no. 8/US 6) knitting needles

Tension/gauge:
26 sts and 26 rows measure 10cm (4in) square over Fair Isle patt on 4mm (no. 8/US 6) needles
IT IS ESSENTIAL TO WORK TO THE STATED TENSION/ GAUGE TO ACHIEVE SUCCESS

What you have to do:
Work main fabric in stocking/stockinette stitch and Fair Isle patterns from charts. Strand colour not in use loosely across back of work. Work top of cover in double (knit two, purl two) rib, making eyelet holes as instructed. Make a twisted cord and thread through eyelet holes.

The Yarn
British Breeds Blueface Leicester DK is 100% pure new wool. Worsted spun for softness, this yarn is one of 10 different breeds offered by British Breed Yarns in a range of natural colours. Blueface Leicester itself is available in 20 colours.

Abbreviations:

beg = beginning;

cm = centimetre(s);

cont = continue;

dec = decrease(ing);

foll = follow(s)(ing);

inc = increasing; **k** = knit;

p = purl; **patt** = pattern;

RS = right side;

st(s) = stitch(es);

tog = together;

WS = wrong side;

yfwd = yarn forward/yarn over to make a stitch

Note:

When working from charts, read odd-numbered (RS) rows from right to left and even-numbered (WS) rows from left to right. Strand yarn not in use loosely across back of work over not more than 5 sts at a time.

Instructions

FRONT:

With A, cast on 59 sts. P 1 row. Cont in patt from chart 1 as foll:

1st row: (RS) K to end, working 1st row from chart 1, working 4 patt sts 14 times across and odd sts at each end of row as indicated.

2nd row: P to end, working 2nd row of chart 1, working 4 patt sts 14 times across and odd sts at each end of row as indicated. Cont in this way from chart until all 12 rows have been completed. These 12 rows form main patt. Work 6 more rows in main patt.

Next row: (RS) With A, k to end.

Next row: With A, p to end.

Now cont in patt from chart 2 as foll:

1st row: (RS) K to end, working 20 patt sts twice across and odd sts at each end as indicated.

2nd row: P to end, working 20 patt sts twice across and odd sts at each end as indicated. Cont in this way from chart until all 19 rows have been completed.

Next row: (WS) With A, p to end.

Cont in main patt from chart 1 until work measures 24cm (9½in) from beg, ending with a WS row and inc 1 st in centre of last row. 60 sts. Cut off B and cont in A only.

Next row: K3, (p2, k2) to last st, k1.

Next row: P3, (k2, p2) to last st, p1.

Work 4 more rows in rib as set. Keeping rib correct, dec 1 st at each end of next 6 rows, then cast/bind off 3 sts at beg of foll 4 rows. 36 sts.

Eyelet-hole row: K3, (yfwd, k2tog, k2) 8 times, k1.

Work a further 5cm (2in) in rib. Cast/bind off loosely in rib.

BACK:

Work as given for Front.

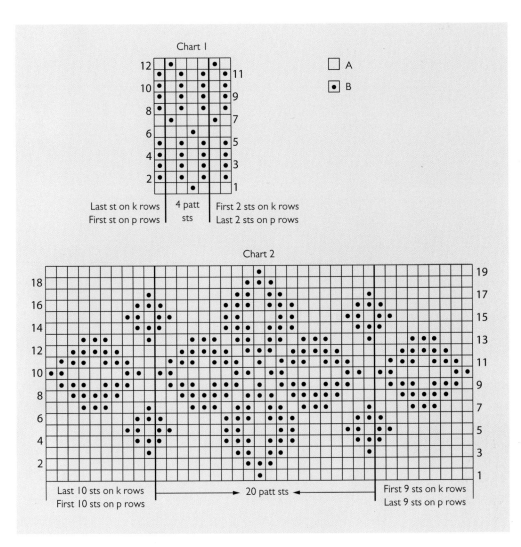

Chart 1

A

B

Last st on k rows
First st on p rows

4 patt
sts

First 2 sts on k rows
Last 2 sts on p rows

Chart 2

Last 10 sts on k rows
First 10 sts on p rows

20 patt sts

First 9 sts on k rows
Last 9 sts on p rows

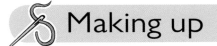 Making up

Press work lightly on WS using a warm iron over a damp
cloth, pressing ribbing only very lightly. Join side seams
and cast-on edges, leaving a gap for tab at base of bottle
if required. With B, make a twisted cord approximately
76cm (30in) long and, starting and ending at centre front,
thread through eyelet holes.

Harlequin draught excluder

Beat the chill with this snazzy design and keep all the family happy!

Worked in an intarsia pattern of colourful harlequin diamonds, this sausage-style draught excluder has circular ends in garter stitch.

GETTING STARTED

Good practise for intarsia colour work as there is no shaping to contend with

Size:
Draught excluder is approximately 91cm long x 11.5cm in diameter (36in x 4½in)

How much yarn:
3 x 50g (2oz) balls of Debbie Bliss Rialto Aran, approx 80m (87 yards) per ball, in colour A – red
2 balls in each of two colours B – orange and C – yellow

Needles:
Pair of 5mm (no. 6/US 8) knitting needles

Additional items:
Washable toy stuffing

Tension/gauge:
18 sts and 24 rows measure 10cm (4in) square over st st on 5mm (no. 6/US 8) needles
IT IS ESSENTIAL TO WORK TO THE STATED TENSION/ GAUGE TO ACHIEVE SUCCESS

What you have to do:
Work main part in stocking/stockinette stitch and harlequin. pattern from chart using intarsia techniques. Work end sections in garter stitch using turning rows to form a circular shape. Fill with toy stuffing to give a rounded shape.

The Yarn
Debbie Bliss Rialto Aran contains 100% merino wool. It is machine washable at a low temperature and there are plenty of fabulous shades to produce exciting colour work.

![instructions icon] Instructions

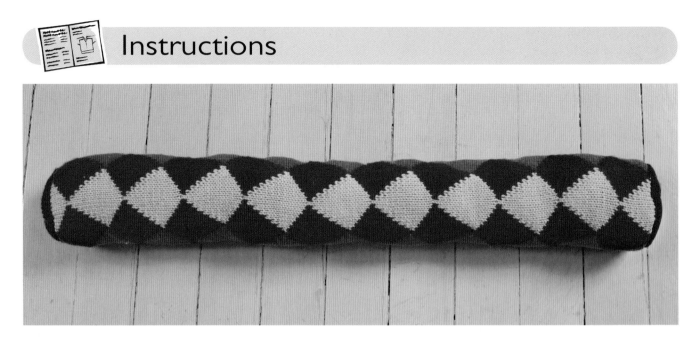

Abbreviations:

cm = centimetre(s);
cont = continue;
foll = follow(s)(ing);
k = knit; **p** = purl;
patt = pattern;
rep = repeat;
RS = right side;
st(s) = stitch(es);
st st = stocking/
stockinette stitch;
tog = together;
WS = wrong side

Note: Before starting work, wind off 4 small balls of A, 3 balls of B and 2 balls of C.

MAIN PART:

With B, cast on 65 sts. Using a separate ball of yarn for each area of colour and twisting yarns tog on WS of work when changing colour, cont in st st and patt from chart as foll:

1st row: (RS) Reading chart from right to left, (k across 32 sts of chart) twice, then work last st as marked.

2nd row: Reading chart from left to right, work first st as marked, then (p across 32 sts of chart) twice.

Cont in patt as set until 22 rows of chart have been completed.

Rep these 22 rows 9 times more.

Cast/bind off in corresponding colours.

ENDS: (Make 2)

With 5mm (no. 6/US 8) needles and A, cast on 10 sts.

1st and every foll WS row: K to end.
2nd row: K9, turn.
4th row: K8, turn.
6th row: K7, turn.
8th row: K6, turn.
10th row: K5, turn.
12th row: K4, turn.
14th row: K3, turn.
16th row: K2, turn.
18th row: K10.

Rep these 18 rows 6 times more. Cast/bind off. Join cast-on and cast/bound-off edges to form a circle. Run yarn around centre sts and pull up tightly to close the gap.

![making up icon] Making up

With RS facing, join long edges of main part, leaving a 5cm (2in) gap in centre of seam for stuffing. Sew end sections in place, matching joining seams. Turn RS out and stuff as firmly as required, then slip stitch opening closed.

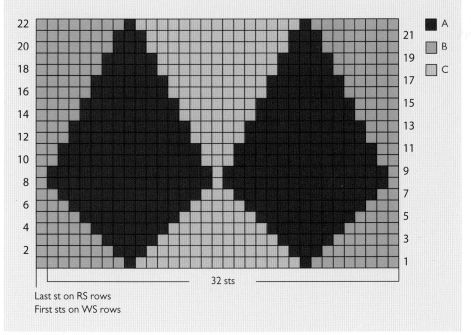

22
20
18
16
14
12
10
8
6
4
2

21
19
17
15
13
11
9
7
5
3
1

A
B
C

32 sts

Last st on RS rows
First sts on WS rows

Polka-dot scarf

Red spots on a white background make a striking scarf that's perfect with a red coat.

Edged in garter stitch, this simple wrapover scarf tucks into the neck of a jacket and has a striking pattern of textured polka dots knitted into it.

The Yarn
Wendy Mode Double Knitting is a practical blend of 50% merino wool and 50% acrylic. It produces a soft fabric with the best qualities of both natural and man-made fibres and can be machine washed at a low temperature. There are plenty of cool pastel and strong contemporary colours to choose from.

GETTING STARTED

Basic scarf is very simple but working polka-dot pattern may take some practise

Size:
Scarf is 83cm long x 18cm wide (32½in x 7in)

How much yarn:
2 x 50g (2oz) balls of Wendy Mode Double Knitting, approx 142m (155 yards) per ball, in main colour A 1 ball in contrast colour B

Needles:
Pair of 4.5mm (no. 7/US 7) knitting needles

Tension/gauge:
20 sts and 26 rows measure 10cm (4in) square over patt on 4.5mm (no. 7/US 7) needles IT IS ESSENTIAL TO WORK TO THE STATED TENSION/ GAUGE TO ACHIEVE SUCCESS

What you have to do:
Work narrow borders at both short ends of scarf in garter stitch (every row knit). Work garter-stitch borders (two stitches) at each end of every row. Make polka dots in contrast colour on every 5th and 6th rows of pattern, stranding yarn across back of work.

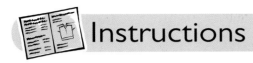 Instructions

Abbreviations:
beg = beginning; **cm** = centimetre(s); **cont** = continue;
foll = follows; **k** = knit; **p** = purl; **patt** = pattern;
rep = repeat; **RS** = right side; **st(s)** = stitch(es);
WS = wrong side

Notes: When working in patt, carry yarn not in use loosely across back of work. Do not twist yarns together at ends of rows as this will show on RS. Instead carry yarn diagonally across back of work to next row of dots. Join in new ball of A 2 sts in from edge of work.

SCARF:
With A, cast on 39 sts.
K 3 rows. Cont in polka-dot patt as foll:
1st row: (RS) With A, k to end.
2nd row: With A, k2, p to last 2 sts, k2.
3rd and 4th rows: As 1st and 2nd rows.
5th row: K4 A, (1 B, 5 A) to last 5 sts, 1 B, 4 A.
6th row: K2 A, p2 A, (k1 B, p5 A) to last 5 sts, k1 B, p2 A, k2 A.
7th–10th rows: Rep 1st and 2nd rows twice.
11th row: K7 A, (1 B, 5 A) to last 2 sts, 2 A.
12th row: K2 A, p5 A, (k1 B, p5 A) to last 2 sts, k2 A.
These 12 rows form patt. Cont in patt until Scarf measures approximately 82cm (32in) from beg, ending with 9th patt row. With A, k 3 rows. Cast/bind off evenly.

 Making up

Sew in loose ends neatly, taking care not to let contrast colour show on RS of work. Press lightly on WS following instructions on ball band.

HOW TO
STRAND THE YARN

The polka dots are worked on the fifth and sixth rows of the twelve-row pattern.

I The polka dots are worked over two rows and are spaced five stitches apart. You need to strand the yarn across the back of the work to keep the fabric flat and smooth and to make the wrong side of the scarf look neat.

2 To begin the first polka dot, join in the red yarn and work one stitch. Pick up the white yarn and work two or three stitches. Take the red yarn across the back of the work and strand it in by taking the white yarn under the red yarn. Continue working with the white yarn to the next polka dot. Drop the working yarn, pick up the red yarn from underneath it and work one stitch. Continue in this way, stranding the red yarn across the back of the fabric and twisting the yarns together to form each polka dot.

Index

Acknowledgements

Managing Editor: Clare Churly
Editors: Jane Ellis and Sarah Hoggett
Senior Art Editor: Juliette Norsworthy
Designer: Janis Utton
Assistant Production Manager: Caroline Alberti